The Power of Laughter

Comedy and Contemporary Irish Theatre

The Power of Laughter

Comedy and Contemporary Irish Theatre

Edited by Eric Weitz

Carysfort Press

A Carysfort Press Book

The Power of Laughter: Comedy and Contemporary Irish Theatre

First published in Ireland in 2004 as a paperback original by Carysfort Press, 58 Woodfield, Scholarstown Road, Dublin 16, Ireland

© 2004 Copyright remains with the authors

Typeset by Carysfort Press
Cover design by Alan Bennis
Printed and bound by Leinster Leader Ltd,
18/19 South Main Street, Naas, Co. Kildare, Ireland

To the comic spirit of Maureen Potter (1925-2004)

Table of Contents

Acknowledgements

I would like to thank the following people and organizations for their contributions to the production of this book:
The National University of Ireland for a grant in aid of publication of this volume; The Arts Council; Karen Fricker and the Irish Theatre Magazine; Mairead Delaney and the Abbey Theatre; John Breen and Yew Tree Theatre Company; Fishamble; Paul McCarthy; Smashing Times; Tinderbox Theatre Company; thanks to Alan Bennis, Carysfort Press, Dan Farrelly, Lilian Chambers and especially Eamonn Jordan; and, of course, all of the contributors.
Eric Weitz

List of Illustrations

Medea: Fiona Shaw (Medea) and Chorus. Photo:
                                Neil Libbert.

That Was Then: Marion O'Dwyer (May) and Stephen
                                Brennan (Noel). Photo: Paul McCarthy.

Kevin's Bed: from left, Sean Rocks (John), Catherine
                                Walsh (Betty), Barbara Brennan (Doris), and
                                David Parnell (Kevin). Photo: Amelia Stein.

Twenty Grand: Liam Carney (Frank Hackett), left, and Karl
                                Shiels (Dean Hackett). Photo: Amelia Stein.

Smashing   Times   facilitated by Paul Kennedy, back
drama workshop:

Barabbas: the early days; from left, Raymond Keane,
                                Mikel Murfi, and Veronica Coburn.

Introduction

Eric Weitz

The title of this collection, 'The Power of Laughter', comes from the name of a short essay written by Sean O'Casey for *Saturday Night*, and collected in *The Green Crow* (1957). The piece celebrates, in O'Casey's lyrically plain-spoken voice, the life-affirming yet inscrutable nature of an everyday bodily eruption that defines our humanity. 'Laughter is wine for the soul', he begins, and goes on to suggest that it serves the species by combating the encrusting tendencies of habit, keeping us fluid and adaptable:

> Man is always hopeful of, always pushing towards, better things; and to bring this about, a change must be made in the actual way of life; so laughter is brought in to mock at things as they are so that they may topple down, and make room for better things to come.

O'Casey has not been the only person to see in laughter a sort of evolutionary payoff for the species, hard-wired in the body for survival the way sexual pleasure ensures continued procreation. Laughter is seen as an instinctive resistance to 'anti-human' lethargy and brittleness, most famously observed by the French philosopher, Henri Bergson, in his 1900 essay on laughter, 'Le Rire': 'We laugh every time a person gives us the impression of being a thing'. At its most spectacular, laughter simulates a sort of bodied earthquake, which lays momentary waste to our encrusted psychic patterns.

'We couldn't live without comedy', O'Casey eventually concludes. He has shifted the emphasis to the other side of the transaction, suggesting comedy as something like the pointed effort to stimulate laughter from a public platform. Indeed, comic genre in the West traditionally displays formal features such as the 'happy ending', but I believe it is fair to say that in most people's minds the term 'comedy', applied to a play, film, or anything else, promises something that will make them laugh.

It is, in fact, the project of all the ensuing essays to hold up for inspection the practices and implications of laughter-provoking strategies and patterns within the general playing field of Comedy and Contemporary Irish Theatre. This is where things get interesting for those of us who, respectfully ignoring all those warnings about dissecting things of ineffable beauty, seek to learn something from a quintessentially human transaction. For more on the unrepentant stance of a comedy head, see Alex Johnston's contribution to this collection, a far-ranging and fearless riff on the practice of comedy. Roughly inspired by the process of conceiving, performing, and reflecting upon his stand-up theatre piece, *Entertainment*, Johnston looks into the heart, mind, and politics of the joking transaction between stage and audience.

Every comic moment in the theatre draws upon a deep, dense root system of experience, which the spectator brings to the theatre event. We know without knowing when a punch line is due; we've been 'trained' to expect laughter in response to certain kinds of performance cues like intonation, physicality, or facial gesture (to the extent that the cue may take prominence over the gag); 'getting' a joke highlights what goes without saying between stage and spectator. It is particularly important to acknowledge that every joke is at someone's or something's expense. This element appears evident in a stage world's pointed jabs of political or social satire. But buxom women and bumbling fathers, for example, have served as time-honoured joking butts for Western audiences, and can to many minds make it seem like *no one* is being laughed at, that, 'It's just good, uncomplicated fun'.

In fact, the comic handling of such material stands to tell us as much about our default cultural codes and prejudices in a single audience reaction as any anthropological study in a thousand hours of fieldwork. This is not to claim that all theatrical joking is by definition sinister or subversive, but to suggest that investigating the many facets of the comic moment in theatre performance shows us a lot about who we are (sometimes more than we'd care to admit), where we've come from, and, no doubt, where we might be headed. Such is the purpose of this book.

The collection brings together essays from the two broad orientations of academic and practitioner, although several of the contributors can be said to swing both ways in this enlightened era of performance studies. (Historically, academics and practitioners have held each other in sniffy distrust, perhaps out of sub-conscious fear that the other might point something out which they really should have considered by now.) The mix of perspectives, manifested in a variety of discursive languages and writing styles, gives a sense of the various issues relevant to comic practice. Looking back over the collection, I believe that each contributor has observed something noteworthy about the workings of comedy, with reference to recent theatre somehow connected to this island and its cultural profiles. By inference, they all also have pointed the way to broader reckonings on the workings of comedy, theatre, and aspects of Western society.

As noted above, 'comedy' is being taken to refer to a theatrical performance, which, among other characteristics, generally obliges itself to elicit laughter. But its uses of humour are also available to other genres, so that 'comedy' or 'the comic' can also appear in tragedy, or in the performance of a tragic text. In this volume, Aoife Monks writes perceptively about the comic slanting of a quintessentially tragic text in Fiona Shaw's turn as Medea, and how it appeared to affect angles of meaning for Dublin and London audiences. Her essay shows us how the operations of comedy point us beneath the skin of performance and reception to the biases informing the transaction, which may well lie beyond the awareness of practitioner and spectator.

Again, comedy and its faithful employee, humour, show more than we realize about our preferences and dispositions, particularly as part of a group. The magic circle of so-called 'insiders' to a given joke may range from two best friends to a tight group of employees to anyone who's read an Irish newspaper in the past several days. Anyone who has lived in another country will attest to the fact that only gradually does one acquire the competence in 'getting' its jokes, and with it brings an exciting sense of inclusion. But as Olabisi Adigun observes in his essay, it is possible to 'get' a joke without laughing at it because the intellectual information is present, but not the emotional disposition. And any culture inscribes its natives from birth with codes that exert a direct bearing on their interaction with other 'humours'.

From a home-grown perspective, Bernadette Sweeney adopts a line of inquiry into comic traditions on the Irish stage, and its various currents and thrusts in the hands of recent (and relatively recent) playwrights, directors and performers. Within and between the lines of her analysis, she reminds us how comedy connects the theatre event explicitly to its time and place, through the spontaneous combustion of material, performance, and audience laughter.

One thing this book will not contain is any attempt to define an essentially Irish humour or comedy. For those who are interested, Vivian Mercier's *The Irish Comic Tradition* (1962) traces a 'cultural continuity' from seeds in Gaelic myth, ritual and magic, to their flowering in twentieth-century writers like Joyce and Beckett. Twenty years later, David Krause sought to forge, at least in spirit, a missing link between Gaelic comic tradition and the Anglo-Irish stage in *The Profane Book of Irish Comedy* (1982). He unearths a Gaelic model for stage comedy in 'The Hidden Oisin', a profane, mock-heroic humour, which he claims is conveniently overlooked by the majority of proud historians and stiff-necked scholars.

It is, in any case, interesting and informative to read Jim Culleton's essay, which contains the insights of six playwrights who have written for his Fishamble theatre company over the past several years. Culleton does us the service of *not* trying to cram everyone under the same banner. He identifies several strains of comic spirit, and invites the playwrights to field their own insights as to how and why they try to make people laugh.

Comedy carries a reputation for serving the status quo. It is common for the group to laugh at the individual who differs, and comedy's generic structure concludes with a reaffirmation of the social order (usually represented by marriage). But several of the essays in this book touch upon comedy's penchant for subversion, perhaps providing new support for sentiments expressed by

O'Casey and Krause. David Grant proposes that a legacy of well-aimed comic trouble-making in the Ulster theatrical tradition – as characterized by Tim Loane's 2002 political farce, *Caught Red Handed* – has sparked communal dialogue on locally taboo subjects where 'serious' attempts fail to break the patterns of stagnation.

The farce-inflected attack discussed by Grant differs substantially from the surrealistic meditation explored by Anne F. O'Reilly in Frank McGuinness's *Innocence*. O'Reilly proposes her own approach to a rarely produced play, which dreams a dark vision of Caravaggio's life as artist and sensualist. By viewing Caravaggio as the 'lord of misrule', she imagines a production funnier and more dangerous than a cursory reading would admit, while retaining the text's brooding interrogations of bodily and spiritual hunger.

In fact, comedy can be seen as far more than seductive – through laughter, it offers a most dramatic way of physically subduing a group of people without touching them. It operates on the body, sometimes prior to intellectual censorship, thereby providing an instrument for the inspection of our own psyches. Jan-Hendrik Wehmeyer looks at a few of the plays of Martin McDonagh with an eye toward this potential for manipulation, asking the morally valid question, 'What are we laughing at and what purpose does it serve?'

This is a question always worth asking. And here is where comedy in contemporary Irish theatre exposes its moorings in a wider European form and technique. In my own contribution to the mix, I look at two National Theatre Society productions – Bernard Farrell's *Kevin's Bed* and Declan Hughes' *Twenty Grand* – both of which drew on time-honoured comic patterns, and through which we might gain an inkling of how an audience 'learns' to laugh via the cultural inscription of dramatic forms.

In many ways, then, a discussion of comedy in an Irish context is a discussion of comedy in a Western context. The post-modern Irish cultural fabric contains swathes of contemporary Hollywood buzz interwoven with traditions of European theatre. Rebecca Wilson unpacks more than just the world according to Martin McDonagh when she looks at *The Beauty Queen of Leenane* through the genre template of melodrama. She advances an intriguing perspective on a hugely popular 'structure of feeling', which our hipper-than-thou culture would consider well past worn.

Where Wilson may be seen to open up an intriguing reinvention of form, Melissa Sihra considers the raw materials of theatre production – the manipulation of the performer's body to spur reflection upon its cultural inscription. She demonstrates, in her essay on Marina Carr's *Low in the Dark*, how defamiliarization of theatrical convention and role-play serves as a potent strategy for comic performance, by 'making strange' the models for gendered behaviour etched on the body by Western culture.

Although practitioners can generally be relied upon to talk for days about what they do on the rehearsal-room floor or in a post-show pub session, it can be rather difficult to get them to commit thoughts to paper. One is not likely to read an essay like Paul Meade's very often, as actors don't readily admit such things about their egos. Yet the alarmingly seductive power exerted by audience laughter, and many a great actor's unceremonious surrender to it, take one right to the core of the chill beneath the thrill in performing with a long-term hit comedy like *Alone It Stands*.

Raymond Keane takes the longer, but no less personal view, in his rumination on clown. Barabbas, the company he co-founded a decade ago and for which he now serves as artistic director, first became identified with their red noses. The clown spirit remains central to its artistic personality – and Keane conducts us past the laughter to the search for truth, which defines the project of comedy for so many practitioners.

Discussions about comic performance often come around to the question of whether such technique *can* be learned to any meaningful degree, or whether it resides in an 'instinct' beyond the command of teaching. Declan Drohan offers a tripartite view – from orientations of student, teacher, and director – on the task of instilling competency in comic practice. The account of his 'journey' centres in each case with experiences in third-level education, with an emphasis on the specific challenges of historical-genre performance.

Finally, the community-based work of Smashing Times Theatre Company relocates the practice of doing things with comedy and humour to more pointedly real-life contexts. Mary Moynihan and

Paul Kennedy show how important such elements become in workshops and performances – primarily involving non-professional artists – as an interpersonal studio tool, and as participants mine their own experiences for the exploration of social issues. Theirs is a different kind of performer-audience dynamic, and their essay observes the humour-driven operations of bonding and recognition in the community-theatre context

Like most notions of nationhood in our globalized, new-century world, the concept of Irishness itself is undergoing whole-sale re-examination. Economic conditions in the wake of the so-called Celtic Tiger, the cultural tug-of-war between the United States and Europe, and the increasingly multicultural face of Ireland are just some of the factors that make 'Irish' a far less telling label than it might once have been. For that matter, the slipperiness of words like 'comedy', 'contemporary', and 'theatre', are such that one could be obliged to spend half a book trying to justify terms of containment and still never fill all the holes. Given the range of work which might deserve to be considered in a book bearing such a sub-title, it is also necessary to acknowledge that the collection cannot be considered complete in any sense of the word. Worthy playwrights, directors, performers and companies – indeed, the realm of Irish-language theatre – have gone unmentioned. The contributors list, too, contains gaps, likely personalities on and around the field of play who would have valuable things to say from any number of analytical and practical positions. Such matters confessed, however, each of the essays does generate compelling points and telling questions from some-where in the vicinity of Comedy and Contemporary Irish Theatre. Taken together, they form a fresh, multi-vocal response to a quintessentially human riddle concerning the practice of theatre and the power of laughter.

1 | Form and Comedy in Contemporary Irish Theatre

Bernadette Sweeney

Comedy is seductive – we like to laugh and to be entertained. Theatre can be perceived as a high art form, too concerned with the meaning of life to spare time for a good laugh. Comedy can seduce audience members into enjoying themselves, however, as evidenced by the comedic strategies invoked in contemporary theatre practice.

> People don't go to the movies to be depressed – that's what *the theatre is for!*

The above quote is from *Stones in His Pockets* by Marie Jones; the section in italics was delivered in performance in the Duke of York Theatre London on 7 July 2003 but does not appear in the published version of the text. This line generated one of the biggest audience laughs of the performance, a seemingly self-aware laugh, metatheatrical, perhaps. But why was this line funny? What is the relationship between the comic content of material and the way in which it is presented in performance? The comic 'value' of dramatic material can be measured most clearly in performance, and can lend an audience an element of complicity, a permission to play, which has, on occasion, pushed the boundaries of theatrical form in Irish theatre.

Irish theatre has a rich tradition of comedy, evident in dedicated comedy and in the darkly comic elements of works by playwrights such as Beckett, O'Casey and Synge. Audiences are moved to laugh at the all-too-familiar despair in the antics of Didi and Gogo in *Waiting for Godot*, at Captain Boyle's self-important posturing in *Juno and the Paycock*, of Michael and his cronies, and the playboy himself, in the *Playboy of the Western World*. These may seem like tired examples, but in each revival an energy and an immediacy emerge from the performance moment, as each generation of actors finds the comedy and contemporary resonance, and brings these to the audiences of the day. In this moment of embodiment actors evoke a visceral response from their audience members indicated, if not quantified, by laughter. And yes, laughter can be as much a nervous response as anything else, but it nonetheless makes real the presence of the audience, and marks key moments of response.

These plays, and others of the canon, include elements of social commentary and satire that were also evoked by such diverse comedies as Boucicault's mid-eighteenth century melodramas and Wilde's late-eighteenth century comedies of manners. Some elements of melodrama transferred later to television, but pantomime developed melodrama's knowing recognition of the presence of the audience. Pantomime in Ireland is not often recognized in studies of the Irish theatre tradition. The Gaiety Theatre in Dublin has a strong association with this theatre form. The venue opened in 1871 with a production of Goldsmith's *She Stoops to Conquer* and staged its first 'panto' *Turko the Terrible* in December 1873. During the mid 1930s, comic actors Maureen Potter and Jimmy O'Dea, especially associated with the Gaiety Theatre, became known for their comic partnership in summer shows and Christmas pantomimes, and did much to establish the immediacy of the theatrical form and introduce its potential to younger audiences. In 1953 Alan Simpson and Carolyn Swift founded the Pike Theatre in Dublin. The Pike ran a series of late night revues and sketches and created a dialogue between these and the work of the main Dublin theatres. These commented satirically on the politics and issues of the day, and referenced the contemporary form in so doing, including, in the words of Pike co-founder Carolyn Swift, 'two compressed pantos of the Jimmie O'Dea and Maureen Potter type – "Red Riding Hood" and "Cinderella" – followed by an Abbey-style "Sean agus an Beano-

Stalk" '.[1] Another such sketch, 'Persecuted People' featured a Communist, a Printer and a Novelist (who was, according to Swift, 'unmistakably Edna O'Brien, who must have been having a rough time with the press just then').[2] These and other details suggest that the Pike was doing for political satire in the 1950s what radio satire *Scrap Saturday*, written and directed by Gerard Stembridge, would do on RTE Radio One in the 1990s.

Comic theatre was not an exclusively urban form, however. From the mid-twentieth century, John B. Keane's work brought a wry comedy to the lives of rural Ireland from his north Kerry perspective. Keane's largely realist work joined the canon through the popular route of the amateur drama circuit. Keane's work, initially rejected by the mainstream, combines an easy wit with cutting social commentary. Keane's comedy is not always kind, but it presents a series of seeming stereotypes, which, while often funny, do not always sit comfortably with audiences. There has been a resurgence of interest in Keane's work, predating his death in 2002, including *Big Maggie* (2001) directed for the Abbey Theatre by Druid Theatre's Garry Hynes with Marie Mullen in the title role, Druid's productions of *Sive* (2002), and *Sharon's Grave* (2003), *The Chastitute* (2002) directed by Terry Byrne with Mick Lally in the title role, and Gemini Productions' *The Matchmaker* (2001), with Anna Manahan and Des Keogh, and directed by Michael Scott. What is particular about Keane's work is his ability to underline even the darkest of dramatic comments with a black, perhaps self-deprecating humour. However, despite the fact that these productions have had the opportunity to invest Keane's work with developments in contemporary form, few of them have substantially extended the theatrical realism of the original works. One of Keane's most significant innovations, if it could be considered as such, was to close the gap between the amateur and the professional theatres.

More recent comic playwrights include Bernard Farrell, who addresses middle-class concerns with plays such as *Kevin's Bed*

---

[1] Carolyn Swift, *Stage by Stage* (1985), extracts from which appear on www.irishreader.com
[2] ibid.

(1998) and *Lovers At Versailles* (2002), and Brendan O'Carroll, who uses elements of pantomime to address working-class concerns with *The Course* (1995) and *Good Morning Mrs Browne* (2001). It is arguable whether their respective audiences can be as easily classified, however. While this work has not been especially challenging in terms of theatrical form, some recent comic theatre has enjoyed a playfulness of form, and a willingness on the part of the audience, not necessarily shared by other theatre performances. This is due in part to the increasing crossover between stand-up comedy and theatre, involving practitioners such as Deirdre O'Kane, Tommy Tiernan, Pat Shortt or Jon Kenny; subject matter where theatre, like stand-up, comments on popular culture, satirizes politics; and an increasing general appreciation of stand-up comedy and comic satire. Some developments offer new perspectives on theatrical form and on the relationship between performer and audience, and suggest that Irish audiences are not averse to passing through the fourth wall.

D'Unbelievables, formed in the early 1990s by Jon Kenny and Pat Shortt, became recognized as 'two of the country's most successful comedians'.[3] D'Unbelievables' work found a place between stand-up comedy and comic drama. Pat Shortt and Jon Kenny, like Keane before them, were firmly fixed in rural Ireland. As D'Unbelievables they toured a series of productions nationally and internationally including *A Bit of a Do* (1992), *I Doubt it, Says Pauline* (1996), and *D'Ats Life* (1999). Recently they have appeared separately but under D'Unbelievable banner. D'Unbelievables built their work around cultural rituals such as marriages, funerals, the GAA and, in so doing, found a way to break through the fourth wall without alienating their audiences. This was a persuasive form of audience participation. Shortt has recognized the significance of this element:

> That's what we do and that's what we are probably known for. We don't just set out to do it for the sake of it. If the character can work with the audience, we'll certainly look at it, but we don't just say 'right, we've got to have audience reaction pieces in the show'. [...] There's no fourth wall in our show [...] Some of the

---

[3] 'D'Ats Life' by Brian Boyd, *The Irish Times* 31 March 1999.

characters will not go near the audience [...] Some of the characters might come down and talk to the audience, but they won't drag them out. They may [...] talk to them as if they're a local person or something like that. But nothing too bad.[4]

Shortt may be underestimating the demands of his work on an audience, however. *D'Video* is a mix of material from different shows, including *It's My Shout*, and *One Hell of a Do*. During a production of *I Doubt it Says Pauline* (at the Limerick Concert Hall in 1996), a series of sketches fitted loosely around the premise of a show at a parish hall due to star themselves, Kenny and Shortt played a series of locals, and addressed directly to the audience, such as a schoolteacher addressing his pupils, or a GAA coach encouraging his team. Under these guises Shortt and Kenny had audience members swapping seats, wandering out of the auditorium having been ordered to close the window, coming onstage to participate in the parish quiz or jumping on Kenny's back during a game of 'Cowboys and Indians'! And, although some audience members might be more comfortable than others at being fair game, the company's growing reputation, and video sales, ensured that later audiences at least knew what they were letting themselves in for. In 1998 Shortt and Kenny appeared in a national tour of the Druid theatre's production of *The Lonesome West* by Martin McDonagh in another crossover between theatre and comedy. Kenny commented, 'The biggest difference we found doing the play was that you must stick rigidly to the text – every word, pause and sentence must be adhered to', and observed that they 'had to un-learn our tendency to improvise or mess around with the material.'[5] While D'Unbelievables' own work may have been uneven in terms of performance or narrative elements, their success in actively engaging their audiences should attest to the power of pleasure in redefining the actor/audience relationship.

Another company notable for engaging audiences through comedy was formed in the early 1990s. Raymond Keane, Veronica Coburn and Mikel Murfi formed Barrabas the Company in 1993.

---

[4] ' D'Unbelievables' by Olaf Tyaransen, *Hot Press*, March 1999.

[5] Kenny quoted in 'D'Unbelievables – D'Story', *The Irish Times* 28 November 1998.

Their mutual affinity for 'jumpy-up-and-down-characters' led them towards 'dedicating a company to eejiting'.[6] Although the company drew from many traditions of physical theatre and comedy they worked most consistently with clown. As described by Keane, 'Clown is a remove from reality, except that, particularly in Barabbas clown we love to mix it with absolute reality and keep that mask of clown, which is somewhat unreal.'[7] By the late 1990s the company decided to tackle the canon, feeling that 'we should do something really Irish, a crackin' Irish comedy, because what we do has a lot of comedy in it, it's what we are.'[8] Barrabas the company first performed *The Whiteheaded Boy* in the Project (then at the Mint), Dublin, in 1997, at the suggestion and under the direction of the aforementioned Gerard Stembridge. In this production the performers developed earlier experimentation with form by moving in and out of character, 'talking to the audience before the show, moving around the auditorium, chatting away'.[9] Barrabas retained this sense of play when it came to performing the actual text. As Keane noted:

> We took Lennox Robinson's stage directions and used them as narrative, speaking to the audience, 'The Whiteheaded Boy, by Lennox Robinson, a well-made play in three acts. Mrs Geoghegan's house is at the end of the street', which is the actual first line in the stage directions. This was another area where we used this 'presentational' form, which I think has the potential to actually invite your audience in a bit more.[10]

Again, comedy was proving a useful strategy in the engagement of the audience, and allowing practitioners to gently extend the boundaries of theatre form.

Gerard Stembridge's work has, arguably, had most impact on radio, with the political satire *Scrap Saturday*, broadcast on RTE

---

[6] Raymond Keane interviewed by Eric Weitz, *Theatre Talk: Voices of Irish Theatre Practitioners* eds Lilian Chambers, Ger Fitzgibbon and Eamonn Jordan (Dublin: Carysfort Press, 2001), p.224.

[7] ibid., p.232.

[8] ibid., p.228.

[9] ibid., p.231.

[10] ibid.

Radio One. However, he is notable for his work as writer and director across the disciplines of theatre, film and television, where he satirizes the politics and urban life of late twentieth and early twenty-first century Ireland. His plays include *Lovechild* (1993), *The Gay Detective* (1996), and *Denis and Rose* (2002). On May 16, 2002, his work made it to the main stage of the national theatre when *That was Then,* written and directed by Stembridge, opened at the Abbey. The play and its Abbey production are significant not only for a satirical reading of contemporary Irish society, but a readiness to play with theatrical form. *That was Then* is set simultaneously in two periods, 'somewhat in the past and slightly in the future'.[11] It also stages two dinner parties and the preparations of same in overlapping physical space, albeit about five years apart. In the 'past', Irish couple Noel and May are out to impress their expected English guests into financing some dodgy property deal. Gombeenism meets the Celtic Tiger as the audience members are invited to look back at our gauche near history. In the 'future' the tables are turned as the English couple June and Julian are in a financial corner and have turned to the newly prosperous Noel for help. Noel now exhibits a sophisticated lifestyle, complete with gorgeous young April in place of May.

In performance, the physicality of the actors changed towards the interval as the interchanges gained speed at the entrances of the guests. Actors physically turned to indicate a comment in the 'past' or 'slightly in the future'. Nick Dunning as Julian was especially shambolic in the 'future' and assured in the 'past' – this elicited laughter from the audience, as did Stephen Brennan as Noel, as he affected the same transitions but in reverse. The physical comedy worked on the premise that characters inhabited each other's space across the time divide, but this was not always effective. Dunning as Julian slumped on the sofa between Brennan as Noel and Marion Dwyer as May; this was one moment where the text was effectively served and extended by the staging: but at another point May and June simultaneously set glasses with napkins on the table, both had hands on each glass at the same time: moments such as these over-stretched the conceit.

---

[11] *That was Then,* Abbey programme note 2002.

Reviewers likened the form of *That was Then* to plays by Ayckbourn, but there are precedents in Stembridge's earlier work including his study of the subjective nature of narrative in *The Truth About Claire*. This 1986 television drama depicted one woman's story from the perspectives of several different characters.

Comedy, as it is seductive, is also lucrative. Irishness, too, sells. *Stones in his Pockets* by Marie Jones opened at the Lyric Theatre, Belfast, on June 3rd 1999. In August of the same year it opened at the Tricycle Theatre, London, and transferred to the West End in May 2000, where it has been running successfully to date. Jones has effected a combination of comedy and social commentary with this play. Two men, in their mid-thirties, are cast as extras when a Hollywood film is shot in a small Kerry village. Actors Conleth Hill and Sean Campion portrayed Charlie Conlon and Jake Quinn, in the early productions of *Stones in His Pockets*, and also took on the play's supplementary roles, such as film director Clem, assistants Simon and Aisling, star Caroline Giovanni and a number of locals. The production, directed by Ian McElhinney, maintained its pared down economical form despite its commercial success – 'poor' values for rich theatre! The two each play a series of characters, and much of the physical comedy emerged from the actors' moments of transition from one role to the next. This sparse casting, while one of the strengths of the production, also yielded weaknesses, as some characterizations were stronger than others. Audiences responded heartily to moments of high energy, such as the Irish dancing scene in Act Two, when the actors managed to portray a number of characters participating together through key gestures and mannerisms, dancing all the while.[12] Another such moment, especially effective in performance, came towards the end of Act One, when the actors nodded their heads vigorously in response to Aisling's instructions:

---

[12] See *Stones in His Pockets*, p.49.

So, when the camera rolls dig until I raise my hand and my hand will be Maeve approaching on the horse…then you will all look up and stare at her…[13]

The script describes the action as follows, but this description and the characters' responses do little to capture the humour of the moment in performance:

They dig…stop…look up…moving their heads as if watching galloping horses and then stop…then look the other way doing the same action. Jake starts to laugh…then can't control himself.

Simon: Cut … yes and what is so funny mate?
Jake: Sorry … it's just hard … you know her hand being Maeve on a horse and your hand being Rory and … (*Laughs*) sorry.[14]

Jones' work has combined some of the elements of popular comic theatre with a commentary on, and conversely a benefit from, the commodification of Irishness. The metatheatrical quote included at the start of this essay evidences the knowingness of this, 'People don't go to the movies to be depressed – *that's what the theatre is for!*' but who is having the last laugh here?

I include *Tilsonburg* as one of the most recent and the most theatrically conservative examples. *Tilsonburg* was written by Malachy McKenna and directed by Liam Heffernan, both of whom appeared in the production. *Tilsonburg* showed its audience members a version of ourselves, or someone at least close to us, as could be judged from the Everyman Palace Theatre audience in Cork. It opened with a very ordinary and recognizable premise – two Irish lads working abroad for the summer. It was a pleasure as an audience member to be amidst such uncomplicated and unadulterated enjoyment, and this was without doubt one of the most responsive audiences I have been a part of in an Irish auditorium – the pleasure of being at something funny. *Tilsonburg* was written with wit and was well pitched to its audience, especially by writer McKenna as Digger and Charlie Bonner as Mac, who played the two main characters with a camaraderie

---

[13] ibid., p.33.
[14] ibid., p.34.

which echoed that of other funny men of Irish theatre, such as Joxer and Captain Boyle, or Didi and Gogo.

Contemporary Irish theatre includes work that is difficult to classify, falling between the gaps of drama, comedy and stand-up. This is where some of the most theatrically challenging work is being produced, as the audience-performer relationship is often pushed outside the bounds of realism. The crossover in terms of practitioners is perhaps one factor in the readiness to explore, and even to participate, on the part of the audience. Is this to suggest that there is a higher level of theatrical experimentation in comic theatre? Not necessarily, but perhaps audiences are more kindly disposed towards experimentation and direct engagement when laughed into it, perhaps even seduced into it, as I stated at the outset. Critic Deirdre Falvey, reviewing D'Unbelievables' *I Doubt it Says Pauline* in 1996, identified the company's 'eye for behavioural detail and wink toward a range of theatrical and comedic styles', but suggested that, 'it would be too po-faced to analyse it thus'.[15] Is there a resistance to a critical analysis of work such as D'Unbelievables'. Is there not room for an interrogation of the comedic strategies invoked in theatre practice? Have I just spoiled the fun?

Sources

Boyd, Brian, 'D'Ats Life', *The Irish Times*, 31 March 1999.

'D'Unbelievables – D'Story' *The Irish Times,* 28 November 1998.

Tyaransen, Olaf, D'Unbelievables', *Hot Press,* March 1999.

Falvey, Deirdre, 'I Doubt it Says Pauline', *The Irish Times,* 4 January 1996.

Swift, Carolyn, *Stage by Stage*, (Dublin: Poolbeg, 1985), extracts from which appear on www.irishreader.com)

Irish Theatre Magazine, edited by Karen Fricker – various issues.

Jones, Marie, *Stones in his Pockets* & *A Night in November*, (Nick Hern Books, London: 2000).

Stones in his Pockets in performance at the Duke of York Theatre, London, 7 July 2003.

---

[15] Deirdre Falvey, 'I Doubt it Says Pauline', *The Irish Times*, 4 January 1996.

Theatre Talk: Voices of Irish Theatre Practitioners ed. Lilian Chambers, Ger Fitzgibbon and Eamonn Jordan (Dublin: Carysfort Press, 2001).

That was Then, written and directed by Gerard Stembridge, produced by the Abbey Theatre, May 2002.

The Whiteheaded Boy written by Lennox Robinson, directed by Gerard Stembridge and performed by Barrabas. Project at the Mint, September 1997.

Tilsonborg written by Malachy McKenna and directed by Liam Heffernan, on tour at the Everyman Theatre Cork, April 2003.

D'Video, D'Unbelievables, Jon Kenny and Pat Shortt, directed by Tom McArdle, Southern Comedy Theatre Production, 1996.

2 | The Outsider: Deborah Warner's *Medea*
Aoife Monks

> Comedy is based on shared experience, attitudes and values; creates
> in-groups and out-groups by mocking aberrations from the norm
> or the norm itself; acts as a form of social control.   (Gail Finney)

Medea is one of theatre's most famous outsiders. The child
murderer and barbarian, the witch and the seductress, Medea has
loomed large in drama, opera, art and literature. Placed in a liminal
cultural position, at the borderline between the domestic sphere
and the public space, Medea transgresses the boundaries of
multiple forms of identity. This lends her a disturbing power as she
inhabits the borderline between masculinity and femininity, insider
and outsider, and public and private.

In Deborah Warner's production of *Medea* at the National
(Abbey) Theatre in Dublin in June 2000, Medea as 'outsider/-
insider' was central to the comedy of the show. While the play is
famous for its harrowing depiction of the murder of children by
their mother, much of the first half of Warner's production
provoked laughter from the audience, and led one critic to suggest
that Fiona Shaw was 'the first funny Medea'.

I want to examine how comedy operated in Warner's production through the relationship between 'insiders' and 'outsiders'
on the stage, relying on a process of empathy and distancing in the
audience for its comic effect. I also want to argue that, in order to
render Shaw's performance funny and ironic, the production relied
on a simplification of the other characters on the stage. I will go

on to examine the London performances of the same show, considering how the change of venue and cultural context influenced the possible meanings the production might have had for its London audiences.

Deborah Warner and Fiona Shaw have been working together in the British theatre since the late 1980s, earning the tag, 'The Terrible Twins', from the British press for their inventive and often controversial approaches to performing canonical texts on the English stage. Warner conformed to a long tradition of adaptations of Greek tragedy in Ireland, when she stated her intention to make the production 'entirely Irish'. She directed the chorus to speak in a combination of English and Gaelic, and a Sean Nós singer sang traditional Irish laments from the audience. Warner's production of *Medea* at the end of the twentieth century in Dublin used the play to engage with the contemporary concerns of Irish culture, coming from her response to a Dublin very different to the one in which she had staged *Hedda Gabler* with Shaw in 1990. As Shaw said:

> The play is very much about a new world that is inquisitive and altering its values. It mirrors a lot of the world one witnesses in Dublin, which is such a boom town that it's quite dizzying. I don't think we are mapping Medea on to Dublin, but it is about a shifting world and I think we're in one.

The production embodied a number of the contradictions and conflicts within contemporary Irish culture, focusing on the family, the abuse of children and the conflict between men and women, and between tradition and modernity. Warner's production constructed an individualist vision of a modern and changing Ireland. In order to engage with these social tensions, the production was structured around a series of oppositions which relied on the simplification of 'traditional' or 'primitive' identities in order to render contemporary and individualist identity (embodied by Shaw's Medea) more complex and interesting in performance.

I want to examine how the juxtaposing of the simplistic with the complex produced comedy on the stage, and how the mechanism of 'laughing with' and 'laughing at' operated within the production. The foreign Medea was positioned as an 'insider' in her relationship with the audience, and the figures styled as 'Irish' were distanced and made less powerful by the aesthetics of the production. Humour was a powerful weapon in the dynamic of this production of *Medea*, and was central to how gender, nationality, and race were imagined on the stage.

Medea at the Abbey

The contrast between the 'private' and 'public' faces of Medea was central to the comedy of Shaw's performance. Below the stage was the private and unseen space of Medea, from which the audience first heard her weeping and raging against Jason's injustice. However, when Shaw first entered the stage, she was unexpectedly muted and embarrassed. The contrast between her private wailing self – reminiscent of her portrayal of Electra in 1988 – and her public understated persona dressed in a black cocktail dress, matching cardigan and high-heeled shoes, resembling an Irish middle-class suburban housewife, created 'at once the unsettling sense of a woman constructing a public self', as described by critic Fintan O'Toole.

Shaw's performance brought the theatricality of Medea to the fore, a theatricality which was integral to Medea's position as a foreigner and as a woman. As Fiona McIntosh suggests:

> [L]ike any other outsider, the rootless Medea has learned that the assumption of new roles is a way of life. But in Medea's case, she comes to see that an ability to perform is really her only guarantee of survival.

Therefore, an evidently artificial persona was central to the irony in Shaw's portrayal of Medea. Tottering slightly on her high heels, and giving the impression that she felt uncomfortable and con-stricted by her clothes, Shaw painted the picture of a woman who was 'playing' at the role of wife and mother, attempting to conform to the social mores of the culture she had adopted, but who was ill at ease with the part she was playing. This gap between the person and the role constructed an ironized relationship between Shaw, the other characters, and the audience, creating a humorous dynamic onstage.

Because Shaw is Irish-born, her Medea's foreignness appeared to be constructed through this ironic gap between person and role rather than through her nationality. This effect was central to Shaw's portrayal of Medea's femininity, which was very evidently a performance and the contradictions, contrasts, moments of self-consciousness and wit, sudden reversals in emotional and physical behaviour and the parodying of feminine roles, such as miming a yashmak when pleading with Kreon, revealed the theatricality of Medea's position on the threshold of Corinthian society. While Shaw played a mother and wife in the production, roles tradition-ally assigned to female characters (and actors), the evident intelligence, self-awareness and wit in Shaw's performance opened up a critique of that role, and of the confining society which forced her to play that part.

The effect of a 'gap' or 'distance' between persona and social role did not only come about through Shaw's performance on-stage. Her public persona as 'actor' also operated within the performance to create a distance between her and her role. Shaw's career has been marked by her engagement with the 'great' canonical roles on the British stage and her Irishness has been configured through her stage roles, positioning her within the British acting tradition of the classical stage. The figure of Shaw-as-actor therefore occupies a liminal national space between English and Irish in publicity and interview material, and this semiotic encoding of her public persona played into Medea's liminality and complicated foreignness in the production. Further-more, Shaw is perceived to be a rigorous, intellectual and fear-somely opinionated actor in interview, with one reviewer describing the experience of interviewing her as, 'like having the top of your head taken off and your cranium scoured out with a brillo pad', and this reputation for intelligence was one lens through which her performance as Medea could be read.

Shaw's public persona as a thoroughly 'modern' ambitious and talented woman operated in her performance of Medea to create a critical distance not only between the 'real' Shaw and her role, but also between the 'fictional' Medea and the social role expected of her. Shaw's self-reflexive humour onstage, her wit and her irony in relation to her lines, worked as a comment on the position of

Medea as foreigner. Her presence as 'modern woman' worked as a counterpoint to the Medea of the ancient world and provided – unintentionally – a critical commentary on the role simultaneous with its performance. The comedy in Shaw's playing was a powerful tool in rendering the outsider Medea an 'insider' within the audience's empathy, ensuring that she became the most sympathetic figure on the stage.

The female chorus members operated in direct contrast to Shaw's performance. Dressed in long, flowing robes and scarves in dark purples, blues and greys, their costumes had an impression-istic similarity to the traditional clothing of Irish women during the famine. They were positioned as an homogenous group of women onstage, an effect which was heightened by the fact that they spoke much of the text in Irish, which worked to exclude Medea from their world. Coupled with the Sean Nós singer in the audience, the styling of the chorus constructed an 'Irish' Corinth which was ancient, undifferentiated and constricting for individual identity. Unlike Shaw's ironical stance, the chorus had humourless, sincere relationships with their roles, and with the audience. This inflexibility formed a stark contrast to Shaw's ironic and humorous presence onstage.

This contrast between the complex foreign Medea and the simplistic, 'Irish' chorus was heightened by the use of the Irish language which had a complicated and paradoxical effect on the stage. Fiona Shaw explained its use in interview:

> I'm just an outsider to a group much more prescribed by design, so that it's very obviously a rather restrictive community; it was almost Islamic wasn't it? [...] In Dublin [the chorus] were heightened versions of local people. [...] The use of Irish is really an extraction [...] it's not that it's Irish, it's that it's a local old language which people use to communicate, it just happens to be a useful tool, and in Dublin what it did is that, if the chorus did speak Irish, the audience understood the local view.

The use of the Irish language was an aesthetic strategy as-sociated with restriction and tradition, but at the same time Shaw presumed that the audience would identify with it and understand it, thus rendering Medea an outsider and the chorus insiders in the affections of the audience. This presumption was somewhat inaccurate, as Dublin audiences are unlikely to speak or understand Irish fluently. The language therefore functioned as a distancing mechanism for them as well as for Medea, becoming an aesthetic flourish which was exoticized on the stage.

Rather than the audience sympathizing with the 'heightened' versions of local people, the reviews and responses from the audience suggested, to the contrary, that the audience identified with Medea, not the chorus, that the Irishness which was attractive on the stage was found in the figure of the liminal, critical and fully contemporary figure of Shaw. The comedy which Shaw created and the chorus did not, may have come out of this difference in identification on the audience's part: the complex foreigner became the figure with whom the audience identified, or aspired to be, while the undifferentiated and superficial 'Irishness' of the chorus was distancing rather than appealing to the audience at the Abbey.

The opposition between a traditional static identity and a modern complex identity, the difference between unfunny and funny, was extended by the male characters in the play. The production maintained many of the popular stereotypes of masculinity, positioning the men as either domineering tyrants or sexual predators. Patrick O'Kane's Jason was characterized by his arrogance and sexuality, swaggering about the stage in a Brando-esque tight, white vest. Jason *was* funny however, his words often provoking laughter from the female audience members, such as his remarks to Medea, when she deceptively apologized to him for her foolishness:

> Well done, my dear/ Not that I blame you for ... before./ It's natural for a woman to be upset./ But now you've learnt: you're sensible./ You took your time, but there we are:/ I was right and you admit it. Well done. (Euripides, 31)

However, unlike the laughter Shaw provoked, the comedy in O'Kane's performance was based on the contrast between his lack of self-awareness and Medea's intelligence, between the one-dimensionality of his characterization and the complexity of Shaw's. Jason was positioned as unknowingly funny, the comedy coming from the combination of his arrogance and innocence.

Unlike the audience's laughter *with* Medea, Jason was laughed *at* by the audience, and the simplistic representations of masculinity functioned, like the chorus, in contrast with the complexities of Shaw's portrait of Medea, ensuring that the audience identified with the liminal, complex and *female* Medea rather than the traditional, static community of the 'Irish' Corinth.

The entrance of Aegeus, the *deus ex machina* character of the plot, established the dynamic of insider/outsider in another way. Aegeus was played by Leo Wringer, an Afro-Caribbean actor, who one critic claimed gave a 'vital injection of colour' to the production. While this may have been unfortunately worded, it is true that Wringer's performance introduced a burst of energy to the proceedings which involved him taking off his red satin coat, stripping to the waist, and conducting a ritual oath by spitting water from the pool into the air and over his body. The energy and display in Wringer's performance was compounded by a moment of comedy, when Medea bargains with Aegeus for sanctuary in Athens, saying, 'Take me in, give me shelter, welcome me./ Your home, my home.' (Euripides, 24) Shaw said the words with a fake Jamaican accent, mimicking Wringer's accent and prompting a laugh from the audience.

The laugh which Shaw's mimicry of Wringer's accent produced came from establishing his difference to Shaw through the markers of race and nationality. The laugh from the audience positioned Aegeus as a comedic figure, something of a buffoon, which was established through Shaw's sign-posting of Wringer's race and nationality. Wringer's black body replaced the more traditional female body as the object of the erotic, and in this case the exotic, gaze. While Wringer's energy and vitality as an actor contributed to the momentum of the production, his performance nonetheless conformed to many of the stereotypes associated with blackness. His appearance within an otherwise entirely white cast, and before a predominantly, if not entirely, white audience, marked his body as an exotic spectacle for the production. Once again Shaw's complex Medea was established in contrast to a simplicity in the representation of other kinds of identity.

Foreignness was central to establishing Medea within a utopian vision of identity which was 'outside' of social constraints and

conditioning. Shaw's status as an 'outsider' in Irish theatre added
to this disjunction between Medea's foreign complexity and the
simplistic renderings of other forms of identity. Even as Warner
used the visual, aural and linguistic tropes of Irishness on the stage,
the production persuaded the audience to reject them in favour of
a transcultural, transcendent Medea. The use of comedy maintained this dynamic, indeed was central to it, ensuring that the
humour of Medea was produced and controlled by Shaw, whereas
the comedy of the other characters came from their contrast to the
complex and intelligent Medea, and the juxtaposing of their simplicity with her complexity.

The production, however, took steps to ensure that the
modern, intelligent and witty Medea with whom the spectators
empathized at the beginning of the production was *not* the Medea
who slaughtered her children at the end. The production employed
a range of distancing techniques to ensure that the audience could
dissociate themselves from the murder and relinquish the empathy
they felt for Medea at the beginning of the play. While Medea the
housewife and mother was an 'inside' sympathetic and humorous
figure, Medea the child-murderer became an outsider, foreign,
strange, distanced and most definitely not funny.

After announcing that she would kill her sons, Shaw as Medea
disappeared offstage, and returned with a white plastic butcher's
apron. Stripping down to her underwear, Shaw put on the apron
and, armed with a kitchen knife, she made her way below the stage
to enact the murder. Once Shaw changed into her butcher's apron
and doused herself with water on the stage, all semblance of
middle-class respectability and decorum were banished from
Shaw's appearance. Instantly, the production signalled a complete
transformation in Medea which allowed the audience to distance
themselves from her actions. The explicit violence of the murder
maintained this alienation effect even further. Paul Taylor described the murder:

> Blood splashes on a translucent screen. One of the sons escapes
> from the blurred side room and runs into plain view, trying to flee
> the fate of his slaughtered sibling. His mother hauls him back.
> After the unbearable tension of the impending atrocity, the
> pressure suddenly drops and insult is added to injury by the sound

of a country and western song that continues with calm insensitivity on a radio somewhere in the building.

Shaw's costume change distanced the audience from their previous empathy with Medea's actions and decision. The change of Shaw's costume, from familiar middle-class naturalism to a brutal abstraction, constructed a new Medea, 'foreign' to the figure with whom the audience had identified, and so the production distanced the audience from Medea's subsequent actions. This was an unfamiliar Medea whose comic presence had disappeared. The production removed any culpability the audience might have felt – through their prior identification with Medea – for the killing of the two boys. As a result, the production relied on an 'inside/outside' mechanism in the figure of Medea herself, where the viewer could identify with Medea and yet reject the possibility that they might be capable of the same crimes.

However, the ending of the play again reconfigured the audience's relationship with Medea. Shaw became identifiable as her original incarnation as the character. Her body language and manner became familiar once more, as she hauled the limp and dangling bodies of her dead sons to the pool of water and began to wash the blood off their limbs. However, her flippant response to Jason's plea to hold his children's bodies, replying, 'request denied', met with no laughter from the audience. The production ended with Medea flicking water at Jason, vainly trying to get his attention once more. Gone was the chariot pulled by dragons, allowing Medea to transcend her crimes, as prescribed by the original text. Instead, Warner's finale was a Beckettian endgame, as Mary Trotter describes: 'This [ending] made the play a parable about both the need for justice and the universally terrible consequences of violent revenge. Warner offered no clear moral winner or loser'.

The anti-climactic ending returned the first incarnation of Medea to the stage, showing her grapple with the consequences of her actions and the futility of the murder. The audience was forced to examine the full cost of the crime, rather than see Medea escape through divine intervention. The production's ending recognized that the murders had solved nothing. By changing the end of the play, Warner maintained her focus on domesticity, but showed that the dramatization of the private sphere of family and sexuality could have devastating consequences for protagonists and audience alike. While Shaw's comic presence had gained her sympathy and 'inside' status in the affections of the audience, the murder and its aftermath forced the audience to confront, in Sarah Iles Johnson's words:

> the disturbing possibility of Otherness lurking within self – the possibility that the 'normal' carry within themselves the potential for abnormal behaviour, that the boundaries that keep our world safe are not impermeable.

Medea at the Queen's Theatre (London)

When *Medea* moved to London, the production retained only Shaw, Wringer and the Sean Nós singer from the original Abbey performances. The recasting of the London production produced a new reading of Medea's foreignness, relying on Shaw's nationality to differentiate her from the British cast. Irishness became foreignness in the London production of *Medea*. This changed the comic nature of the production, rendering the playing of Shaw less humorous, and reconfiguring the power relations on the stage.

The styling of the chorus was radically altered in the London production. Played by English actors, they were dressed in contemporary clothing and resembled housewives, students and business women. Not only were their costumes differentiated, they now moved with individual body language, accentuated the differences in their regional accents, and were blocked naturalistically on the stage. The chorus members were now humorous on the stage, provoking laughs from the audience due to the contrast between their normality and familiarity and the heightened emotional circumstances of their presence onstage. Rather than presenting the chorus as an homogeneous group of 'local women,' the production instead positioned them as a collection of different kinds of women, creating a sense of diversity and multiplicity in the local England/Corinth. The London production presented an English chorus who were styled to appear contemporary, diverse and individuated unlike the Irish chorus in the Abbey.

Shaw's portrayal of Medea also changed. Fiona Shaw's Irishness was emphasized by this production. The recasting of the show meant that Medea's foreignness was established through the accident of Fiona Shaw's birthplace. Now, Irishness was founded in accent and biography, and became an essence which was defined through origins and accent. This meant that there was less critical 'space' between Shaw and her role, the production relying on biography as a means to establish identity. Shaw's own performance of Medea also changed, placing more emphasis on the high emotional stakes of her performance rather than on the subtle nuances of irony and wit which had characterized her performance in Dublin. Medea the housewife and Medea the murderess were brought closer together in this production and the critics noted the histrionic aspects to Shaw's performance.

The character of the nurse was also played by an Irish actor, and Fiona Shaw addressed her in Gaelic. While the production retained the use of the Irish language, the intention behind its use was transformed, as Shaw explained:

> Here [in London] I am just using a tiny fragment, [because] she might revert to a language that the chorus wouldn't understand, that the audience wouldn't understand, which is fundamentally not so sympathetic, because people don't like not understanding things.

The intention behind the use of the Irish language reversed in function: moving from being (supposedly) inclusive of the Irish audience, but excluding Medea in Dublin, to becoming an effect which meant to exclude everybody *but* Medea and the nurse in London. This new usage relied on the defamiliarizing effects of the language, and so Irishness became part of a menacing foreignness, figured as strange, exclusive and unreadable, gaining what Warner described as 'that threatening quality'. Medea was positioned as far less sympathetic to the audience in the London production. Shaw's overstated acting had an alienating effect, and her use of Gaelic created the possibility that her deceptiveness to Jason and Kreon might extend to her relationship with the audience. Shaw's performance was far less funny and was furthermore placed in opposition to an individualized, contemporary English chorus. Medea's foreignness did not position her as a critical, complex figure – now it was an 'insider' Englishness which was endowed with these qualities. As with the Dublin production, Irishness was associated with exclusion and tradition. However, while the aesthetics of Irishness remained the same, the London production reversed their meaning, transforming them into the markers of the 'foreign' and the 'outsider,' rather than signifying the (insider) Corinthian establishment.

While Wringer's performance was similar to the Dublin production, his scene with Shaw took on a new meaning. Aegeus' and Medea's foreignness within an 'English' Corinth, was reflected in the figures of a Jamaican Wringer and an Irish Shaw acting in the 'Queen's Theatre' in London. Wringer and Shaw's outside status as actors became more visible and established a greater sense of equality between the characters than in the Dublin production, which had established Shaw as more powerful than Wringer. This new-found equality was maintained by the fact that, in an earlier scene, the tutor had mockingly mimicked the (Irish) nurse's accent, asking her, 'What wrongs are you muttering this time?' This scene pre-empted the mimicry of Wringer's accent, and Irishness and Jamaican-ness were both comically established as Other to the dominant voice onstage. Shaw and Wringer re-presented sympathetic characters with whom the audience could identify, and simultaneously provided distance as Other: Wringer as the exotic black man, and Shaw as the murderous Irishwoman.

Warner and Shaw's production of *Medea* offered a contradictory approach to identity on the stage. While on the one hand they worked in the same mode as previous Irish *Medeas*, by using the Greek tragedy to explore contemporary Ireland, they nonetheless eschewed any identity that seemed to be defined by Irishness. Instead, they favoured an individualism which could transcend the institutions of gender, race or nationality. Fiona Shaw's bravura and complex performance relied on a simplification of other identities and performances on the stage. Nonetheless, her performance had a powerful and important effect both in Dublin and in London. The murder scene and its aftermath visibly shook audience members who were forced to acknowledge their complex and problematic social attitudes towards children and family. In its unwavering gaze at the extreme results of betrayal, and by creating a critical, ambiguous, funny and sympathetic Medea, this production forced its audience to confront the terrible politics of home.

Sources

Chillington Rutter, Carol, 'Fiona Shaw's *Richard II*: The Girl As Player King As Comic', *Shakespeare Quarterly,* vol. 48, 1997, no.3.

Euripides, *Medea,* trans. McLeish Kenneth, Raphael Frederic, Nick Hern Books, London, 1996.

Finney, Gail, ed. & Introduction. 'Unity In Difference', *Look Who's Laughing: Gender And Comedy,* University California Davis, Gordon & Breack, USA, Switzerland, Australia, Belgium, France, Germany, Britain, India, Japan, Malaysia, Netherlands, Russia, Singapore, 1994.

Johnson, Sarah Iles,'Introduction', *Medea: Essays on Medea in Myth, Literature, Philosophy and Art,* James Clauss, Sarah Johnson eds (Princeton, New Jersey: Princeton University Press, 1997).

McCarthy, Gerry, *The Sunday Times,* 30 April 2000.

McIntosh, Fiona, 'Introduction: The Performer To Performance', *Medea In Performance 1500-2000,* eds Edith Hall, Fiona McIntosh & Oliver Taplin, (Legenda, European Humanities Research Centre, University Of Oxford, 2000).

Meaney, Helen, *The Irish Times,* 27 May 2000.

O'Toole, Fintan, *Irish Theatre Magazine,* Volume 2, Number 6, Summer 2000.

Shaw, Fiona, interview with the author, London, February 2001.

Taylor, Paul, *The Independent* (English), 8 June 2002.

Trotter, Mary, 'Performance Review, *Medea*', *Theatre Journal,* Vol. 52, No. 4, December 2000.

Whitley, John, *Daily Telegraph,* 24 March2000.

3 | *Alone It Stands*: 'How I Learned To Crave Laughter and Other Secrets of a Touring Player.'
Paul Meade

> Now this overdone or come tardy off, though it makes the unskilful laugh, cannot but make the judicious grieve; the censure of the which one must in your allowance o'erweigh a whole theatre of others…

> …for there be of them that will themselves laugh, to set on some quantity of barren spectators to laugh too, though in the mean time some necessary question of the play be then to be considered; that's villainous, and shows a most pitiful ambition in the fool that uses it. (*Hamlet*, Act III, Scene ii.)

The above passage from Shakespeare's *Hamlet* forms part of what is commonly known as 'the advice to the players'. This essay attempts to show how that advice might apply to a modern-day 'fool' who, thinking it was his job to make people laugh, got a little confused along the way. That 'fool' was me as I toured Ireland and the world in John Breen's rugby comedy *Alone It Stands*.

I first saw *Alone It Stands* at the Belltable Arts Centre in Limerick and like the other audience members around me I laughed myself into submission. The play, performed by only six actors on a bare stage, tells the story of Munster beating the mighty All Blacks in Limerick City in 1978. The six actors portrayed over sixty characters and a whole rugby match in a very funny, very physical show.

The actor who stood out for me that first night, partly because I had never seen him perform before, was Conor Delaney. It seemed that he had walked out of a cartoon and landed on the stage. He played a dog that you wanted to pet, a super-fast fullback in perfect slow motion, a twelve-year-old kid with the bandiest legs I am ever likely to see, and about seven other equally impressive characters. Throughout, his timing, his physicality and his rubber face provided a master class in comic performance.

That was October 1999. In April 2000 I received a call from my friend and fellow Limerickman, John Breen, whom I had met when I first started college in Dublin. Would I help him out? One of his actors was down and could I step in for a few weeks while he recovered? As out-of-work actors are prone to do, I said yes almost immediately, despite the fact that the incapacitated actor was Conor Delaney and I had only one week's notice.

One week's notice. That did not translate into one week's rehearsal. In fact, outside of watching the show, learning lines and practising the Haka (a Maori war-dance used by the All Black team to intimidate opponents) in my bedroom, I was afforded the equivalent of three days rehearsal time. I did what any sane person would do: I tried to imitate Conor Delaney. I had what I thought was a piece of gold – the video of Conor actually playing the part – and I remember a sweaty few hours before my first performance in the Gríanan Theatre in Letterkenny, pressing FAST FOR-WARD and REWIND over and over again on the video machine in the green room. I tried to imitate Conor's performance move for move, gesture for gesture.

That night the rest of the cast pushed and pulled me through my first show. There were frantic whispers: 'What's next?', 'Line Out', 'Which one?', 'Just follow me you fool!' That sort of on-the-spot side-coaching thing is easy in *Alone it Stands,* as the regularity of the laughs and the volume of the onstage cheers allow for all sorts of chat. I would later find myself in that position of onstage director, pushing a fellow actor into a scrum or a maul and hoping they would still speak to me later. Back then I was quite happy to be manipulated like some sort of puppet version of Conor, and it got me through. Just before the curtain call I had a horrible feeling that I may have ruined the show for everyone. These guys had been getting standing ovations for six months straight; would I be responsible for ending that? I needn't have worried – the crowd rose to their feet to applaud us and I felt an enormous sense of relief. I had cracked it.

Or had I? I was recalled as a super sub once again the following June when Conor sustained another injury. We rehearsed a little more thoroughly this time (though not much) and I did a week in Dublin before we headed for the Edinburgh Fringe. It was during our run at the Traverse Theatre in Edinburgh that all my feelings of security and contentment in my role began to vanish. It started slowly. Some laughs that I had been getting weren't always there. For instance, a mention of Consulate cigarettes normally elicited a laugh of recognition that these were a particularly mild brand. I tried to think about the line, my physicality and my delivery. What was I doing wrong? I factored in the fact that this was the first non-Irish audience I had played to and that some of my lines referred to culturally specific items like Major cigarettes and Red lemonade. The whole play, I began to think, works best with an Irish audience and their laughter is a laughter of recognition. A horrible thought: maybe the 'Irish' factor had papered over the cracks – of which I was one.

Other events in Edinburgh further dented my confidence in what I was doing. Firstly, we received a less favourable response from the Scottish papers than we had received in Ireland. Yes, I do read reviews. My imagination writes far worse criticism than any reviewer and I like to know what everybody else knows. I never allowed the reviews to change what I was doing, and none of them mentioned what was a very tight ensemble individually, but they contributed to a vague sense of self-doubt that hung over me. I felt like second choice, a pale shadow of Conor, a stop-gap, a filler, a substitute.

Another factor started to worry me during our stay in Edinburgh. When I first took over from Conor in Donegal, I was the only new cast member. The rest of the cast had created the show with John over a five-week period the previous September. Now in Edinburgh there were only two original cast members left. I began to miss things that I hadn't even realized were there before; a groan here, a shout there, an injection of pace or energy at the right moment, a noise that covered an uncertain moment. These were things that you couldn't learn, that weren't in the script. These moments had been created by the actors, they were part of the show but they had never been annotated in any way. How do you pass on a myriad of looks and gear changes and vocalizations? In the Irish system of theatre only the most basic moves are recorded in the stage manager's book and once the actor leaves, he or she doesn't stay on to bring the new performer through the show. *Alone it Stands* is a physically tiring show and people want to spend the minimum amount of time in the rehearsal room. So we achieved the basic shape of the show and were happy with that. I began to feel that something was missing because of this, but I didn't know how to get it back.

I should say that we finished our run in Edinburgh to packed houses. We had drama students coming up to tell us that this was the best show they had ever seen in their lives, and we had sold out a three-week run back in Ireland. The show was still a massive success. All my niggling doubts must surely have been the neurotic musings of a perfectionist. A pilot once told me that every time he got in the cockpit he believed he could improve on what he had achieved during the previous flight. That's how he kept his concentration and his focus. I think acting can be compared to flying a plane: you must constantly seek to improve or you will fall out of the sky.

The next December I got what I thought would be my chance to improve on all the mistakes I was making in Edinburgh. We were rehearsing for two weeks prior to a long tour of Ireland and then a three-week tour of Australia. When I came down from dreams of our trip to the International Festival of the Islands in Tasmania, I resolved that I would use these two weeks of rehearsal to re-investigate the moments in the play that were troubling me. Unfortunately I forgot that rehearsals weren't designed to facilitate the pet project of any particular member of the cast. We had two new players and they needed every available second. John also had plans for a revised ending and a new 'funny' Haka. In *Alone it Stands* alongside performing the traditional Maori Haka we also acted out, like the New Zealand team of 1978, a satirical version of the Haka. John spent a large proportion of those two freezing weeks in December developing a funnier version of what we had been doing in Edinburgh. It seems I wasn't the only one intent on improving things. Indeed, as the years went on (*Alone it Stands* is entering it's fourth, as of this writing), I realized that everyone in the cast was intent on improving the show in whatever way they could, and given the resources and time we would have quite happily spent months in rehearsal getting the show 'right'. The result of those two weeks in December, however, was a much-improved 'funny' Haka, two new cast members who knew the show – and no respite from my real or imagined 'problems'.

After a long, hard tour of Ireland we flew out to Tasmania. Here in a foreign land the spotlight would shine once again on any deficiencies in the play and the performances. What should have been cause for celebration – packed houses of Australians were laughing their socks off at a play that we thought peculiarly Irish – became a cause for concern in our glass half-empty world. We began to concentrate on the laughs that we weren't getting and forgot about the new laughs that had arrived (in some cases due to the fact that New Zealanders are to Australians what Kerrymen are to the Irish, and that they took every opportunity to laugh at the antics of the All Black team of '78). We found ourselves looking at brand names again and John decided to change some of them. Major cigarettes became Rothman's and a Ford Granada became some kind of Australian car. We started saying Garryowen Rugby Club instead of just Garryowen and our Limerick accents had to be toned down and become more intelligible. I found that particularly hard. As the only Limerickman in the cast, the accuracy of my accent allowed me some comfort when laughs were in short supply.

The culture gap between us and the audience left some moments of 'dead air' on the stage. Where once there had been a 30-second laugh, there was silence. We called these instances of deafening non-laughter 'tumbleweed moments', after those scenes of quiet tension in Hollywood Westerns where there is silence, a bell tolls, and tumbleweed rolls across the street. Late one night in an Irish bar in Hobart, Tasmania, we tried to judge who was king of the tumbleweeds. Dessie Gallagher did a fantastic impersonation of me desperately trying to ring a laugh out of the line, 'Good man yourself', and I was dubbed 'Tumblemeade'. Only then did I realize how far I had fallen.

I had become hooked on laughs. 'Good man yourself', had brought the house down regularly in Ireland, believe it or not. In Australia there were embarrassed titters for a man who was making a fool of himself onstage. I was like a junkie looking for a fix, elongating the line, deepening my voice, adding colour. I would have tried anything short of dropping my trousers. After Dessie's late-night intervention I realized that the audience were, at least subconsciously, aware of my efforts to extract a laugh from them and I contented myself with just saying the line. Thinking of Hamlet's advice I can only conclude that the Tasmanian audience are, in the main, judicious, that I was villainous and that my performance was completely o'erdone.

Back in Ireland I regained my composure when the laughter started to flow more regularly but still I had questions. Was there a better way of recognizing problems and of solving them than late-night banter in a pub? How could we retain the precision of the show and its original integrity over such a long period of time and with so many cast changes? I hit upon a very obvious and perhaps dangerous solution. Why didn't we look at the original video? Great idea, except no one could find it. The next couple of times we rehearsed I repeated the same mantra, let's look at the video. People agreed and promises were made to call this person and that, but no one seemed to have a copy. I just had to let it go.

But I was still struggling with those few moments that I couldn't get right. Here's an example: In this scene there are four of us playing kids preparing for a bonfire. Spider, the leader, asks Dandy what he has acquired by way of flammable materials. Dandy gives Spider a long, long list of various bits of wood, etc., which he has gathered. Then Spider turns to me and asks for my list. I answer, 'Four firelighters.' When I first took over from Conor that line always got a laugh; now, three tours, three different rehearsal periods, and three different Spiders later, and with the odd month off here and there, I couldn't get that laugh back. I knew it had something to do with looking at Spider, then looking at Dandy, then back at Spider and then saying the line, 'Four firelighters' and stressing 'lighters'. Still it would come and go. I wasn't sure. I saw the same syndrome in the other actors. If they just upward inflected that line, if they ran those two words together like they used to, a pause here, drop the pause there, it's so easy from the outside. So I kept trying and one day they would laugh and the next they wouldn't. It was infuriating.

The show kept going, we played ever bigger houses, the Gaiety and the Olympia in Dublin, the Cork Opera House. People came to the show four and five times. We got standing ovations; people cried with laughter. In some ways the show just got better and better. But still we all scratched our own itches. John kept changing the ending trying to get it right. He kept rehearsing the moment where one of my characters gets tackled (a painful experience once a night, excruciating ten times a day in rehearsal). And I kept thinking, 'Spider, now look at Dandy, then back, maybe I held it too long – Doh!' During this period we visited the Duchess Theatre in the West End of London. And John cracked the ending! We had always sung the Limerick rugby anthem, 'Alone it Stands', as a rousing finale to the show, but John was continually looking for a good reason for us to sing the song. The solution lay in having the character of Gerry use the song as a way of convincing his friend Lanky that it was okay that he had been forced to call his two boys 'Garry' and 'Owen' after a rival rugby club. It sounds silly but it worked. That was one down. After London we had a three-month break in which to dwell on things.

In rehearsals for the next tour the video finally reappeared. One day we all sat down to watch it. I knew what I was looking for and I found it. It's the same sequence of looks that I described above, the same rhythm that I remembered when I first saw Conor perform the role – but watching the video of his performance helped me enormously. Even though I always understood the anatomy of that moment I realized that I had begun to mistrust it. Over time the variations in audience response eroded my confidence in what I was doing. Instead of trusting my rehearsed choices, I allowed ever-increasing 'improvements' to creep into my performance.

So, I gained new confidence from looking at the video but I also heightened my awareness of the meaning behind the looks to Spider and Dandy. What I saw in the video was Conor looking at

Spider with horror as he realized he would be asked to account for his share of the bonfire. Then Conor looked at Dandy for support only to realize that Dandy had increased the pressure on him by having acquired so much bonfire material. The fun lay in Conor's anticipation of Spider's disapproval. His look to Dandy allowed the audience to see a man frantically searching for a way out. Observing Conor's actions allowed me a deeper understanding of the thought process behind his movements. I now believed I understood this troublesome moment, instinctively and consciously, only performance would be the test of whether I was right.

Rehearsals continued and I resisted rehearsing the tackle again. Mainly for health reasons, but John, determined, patient and insistent, wore me down. In one sense the tackle works like a big pratfall. The audience needs to be able to imagine the pain in order to laugh. Twenty tackles and a very sore back later we cracked that as well. Things were really coming together.

In front of an audience the difference was audible, I got an immediate response to 'four firelighters' and the tackle got a gasp and then a laugh. Maybe about a year too late for my fragile comic ego, but it was still a pleasure. I also had the ability to sustain it over the four-month period of that run, and as a group we just tuned the show tighter and tighter and tighter. The show was a pleasure to do. It felt right and enjoyable; we were no longer scrabbling around in the dark, we were confident and working like a team. I really believe that watching the video contributed to that, and I know it helped me. Then again, we finished that leg of the tour only four months later and with no cast changes. There is every reason to suspect that time, cast changes and the varying responses of audiences could contribute to a running down of any well-oiled machine.

Having hung up my rugby boots for the time being, looking back on two and a half years as a substitute proved to be sobering. I feel a certain empathy with Shakespeare's fools and players as I am even more aware of the pressures and conditions that could cause them to alter their performances to the detriment of the play they were performing. My playing was very slowly altered by audience response and the lack of audience response, by reviews and by comments from peers. I felt under an obligation to be funny as I was not the original creator of the role and this accentuated my sensitivity to all these factors. I understand how the pressure of a short rehearsal period and constant cast changes can affect the quality of a show. I know how difficult it can be to hold on to the truth of a piece in the face of a constantly changing audience with different demands, different levels of understanding, different reactions. I realize that no performance piece can ever be passed on intact from one performer to another. A script cannot capture every gesture, a prompt book cannot accurately describe each individual performer, and even seeing a show live leaves us with the question, 'What happened last night?' Performances are elusive, changing things and anything can happen on any given night. Hamlet admits as much when he says, 'let those that play your clowns speak no more than is set down for them'. But I can't help thinking that, like this clown, Shakespeare himself would have killed for a video.

4 | Breaking the Circle, Transcending the Taboo
David Grant

It is the middle of the second half of the opening performance of Tim Loane's *Caught Red Handed* (9 February 2002). We are sitting in the old Assembly Rooms of Belfast. Most recently a branch of the Northern Bank, this building, at the heart of the city's historical mercantile centre, had played host 210 years earlier to the Belfast Harp Festival, prompting Wolfe Tone's memorable critique – 'Strum, strum, strum and bedamned!'.

And yet, for Edward Bunting and the other organizers of the Festival, the reclamation of the harp, like the reclamation of the Irish Language, was a dissenting and a radical act. These were the symptoms of a brief Belfast flirtation with the Enlightenment. The winds of change were blowing from east and west, from America and France. Tom Paine was a household name. And in only six years, following the failure of the United Irishmen, Henry Joy McCracken, a Protestant radical Belfastman, would be hanged in Belfast's Cornmarket. This would inspire another Protestant radical Belfastman, Stewart Parker, to write *Northern Star* nearly two centuries later, which yet another even more radical Protestant Belfastman, Stephen Rea, would direct for Tinderbox Theatre Company in the historic Rosemary Street Presbyterian Church to mark the bicentenary in 1998 of McCracken's execution. Four years later we are in another historic building which has been pressed into temporary use by the same enterprising theatre company for the premiere of Tim Loane's first stage play. He, too, is a part of that radical Protestant tradition. But this time, the play, *Caught Red Handed*, is a satirical comedy.

The actor, Peter Ballance appears on the stage. The video screens, which are an integral part of the production concept and which have served to evoke the significance of media inter-pretation on our understanding of Ulster politics, suddenly become the monitors in an imagined television studio. Among the first night audience, David Dunseith, presenter of BBC Northern Ireland's television discussion programme *Let's Talk*, finds himself confronted by a ghastly alter ego – the exaggerated presenter of the fictional *Let's Chat*. Up come the lights on the audience, shattering our sense of safe detachment from the action on the stage before us. And we are asked to raise a hand if we would be in favour of a United Ireland. There is a frisson of discomfort, and then an uncharacteristically shy smattering of response. It is an exceptionally effective moment of theatre, as the sacred contract of 'suspension of disbelief' that traditionally governs the relation-ship between audience and actors is subverted. This is a comedy, and the dilemma we are being faced with is undoubtedly funny. But it is also uncomfortable.

In this moment, the political detachment which for decades has characterized the chattering classes which populate such occasions as theatre first nights is peculiarly challenged. We are exposed – and forced to confront the political realities which for the most part we are able to ignore. It is to prove the most politically in-cisive moment of the performance, the payload of the evening delivered in its apparently silliest scene. Audience participation is always discomforting for its victims, but on this occasion the effect goes beyond mere embarrassment. Our status as detached ob-servers had been challenged. And all the more tellingly because that challenge comes in the middle of a largely farcical comedy. Our defences are down.

Detachment as a means of defence has been a familiar strategy in Northern Ireland. Carlo Gebler has written memorably about the way in which we tend confidently to assure visitors here that trouble is restricted to certain towns, and in those towns to certain estates and in those estates to certain streets, and in those streets to 'the house with the blue door'. We all, he concludes, live in the house with the blue door. Damian Gorman identified a similar phenomenon when he wrote in his 1992 verse drama for the BBC about 'devices of detachment', which in his view are as deadly as the more familiar and ominous 'suspect device', a common euphemism for a possible terrorist bomb:

> I've come to point the finger
> I'm rounding on my own
> The cagey decent people
> I count myself among ...
> We are like rows of idle hands
> We are like lost or mislaid plans ...
> We're working under cover
> We're making in our homes
> Devices of detachment
> As dangerous as bombs.

Gorman's fine documentary confronted us directly, in the lead-up to the 1994 IRA ceasefire, with the collective responsibility we all shared for the continuing violence – but significantly he used a vehicle aimed mainly at a school audience. Nearly a decade later, a different approach seems necessary to reach a still-resistant general public. Comedy has the capacity to circumvent the deep-seated defences to which Gorman alludes.

Set in 'Belfast, Northern Ireland/The North of Ireland/The Six Counties/Ulster 2005 AD', *Caught Red Handed* opens with a news report announcing the imminence of a referendum on a united Ireland, and proceeds to explore the impact of this announcement on the leadership of the Alternative Unionist Party. Its most immediate consequence is the untimely death of the party Leader, prompting his closest associates to contrive an elaborate deception and to substitute a lookalike for their deceased chief in order to avoid a disastrous leadership tussle at so sensitive a time for Ulster Protestantism. Apart from presenting copious opportunities for good gags, this device also provides a marvellous double-role for the versatile actor, Dan Gordon.

To this extent the plot echoes the 1993 movie, *Dave*, in which an employment agent with a social conscience is persuaded by White House aides temporarily to replace the President of the United States. But whereas in the film, the demands of realism give rise to feel-good romanticism, the theatricality of the stage equivalent propels events into a welter of broad farce. Although not primarily a political film, *Dave* does provide a platform for a certain kind of Hollywood liberalism. *Caught Red Handed* uses the liberating power of live comedy to grapple much more directly with the political themes inherent in the plot. In style, and in its level of political engagement, it is reminiscent of the work of Dario Fo, one of whose plays, *Can't Pay, Won't Pay*, Loane directed for Tinderbox in September 1992.

The political significance of the theatre status as a live event is evident in the *Let's Chat* moment described above. The cinema screen cannot (yet) directly call its whole audience to account and expect a response. Even given the possibilities of digital interactivity, no electronic connection can ever exert the same influence as the living presence of an actor standing only a few feet away. To that extent, *Caught Red Handed* does no more than illustrate classic Brechtian theory in confronting the audience with the issues in which the play deals, and demanding an engaged response. But I have rarely felt so directly and personally under scrutiny during a live performance. The play's secret weapon was its use of comedy to allow the direct address of issues, which for all their currency are still, in practice, largely taboo.

I am reminded of the experience of seeing the 1975 Lyric Theatre production of Patrick Galvin's *We Do It For Love*. After half a decade of civil disorder, this production explicitly brought politics to the stage through the medium of (often very black) comedy. Many outsiders, were shocked not so much by the substance of the play itself, but by the unrestrained hilarity of the local audience members around them. As late as 1979, a similar bewilderment was evident in 'mainland' response to Ron Hutchinson's television drama, *The Last Window Cleaner*, which attempted to bring a similarly irreverent approach to the Northern Ireland situation before a nationwide audience. Every time the eponymous window cleaner approached a window to clean it someone threw a stone through it. His family survived the economic strictures of the Troubles by systematically mutilating an elderly relative and then claiming compensation for his injuries. They also let out rooms to a sado-masochistic gay couple who crossed the screen periodically taking it in turns to be prisoner and interrogator. Despite its relentlessly satirical tone, the response in Great Britain ranged from mystification to outrage. But in the throes of some of the worst violence of the last thirty years, the 1975 Lyric audience lapped up Patrick Galvin's satire.

We Do It For Love is a cross between music hall and Lehrstück (the Brechtian notion of a 'learning play'). It opens with a fairly explicit acknowledgment of Joan Littlewood's *Oh What a Lovely War!* with soldiers singing, 'I don't want to go to Belfast', to a tune associated with the Great War. In subsequent scenes, rival gunmen engage in a vaudevillian double act, bombers sing and dance, and archetypal women from the opposing sides exchange abuse. The only truly happy character is the undertaker. The soldiers are presented just as much as the victims of the situation as the hapless bystanders. The published text ends with 'An Additional Finale' (a testament itself to the demand for encores) with the lines, 'I want to leave old Belfast city/And join the human race'. In the face of despair, comedy provided a glimpse of hope. While there were some dissenting local voices (such as a letter from the *Belfast Telegraph* letter's page, headlined, 'Lyric play's portrayal of RUC men "unfair and unforgivable" '), the play was an undeniable triumph, being first extended and then rapidly revived for touring.

In much the same way as the general phenomenon of the Troubles proved a difficult subject for dramatists to come to terms with in its early years, so, too, the more problematic aspects of the Peace Process have been slow to find serious expression on the stage. In particular, the unresolved dilemma of how to reconcile disaffected members of the Protestant community remains something of a taboo. Gary Mitchell has come to prominence as a representative voice of one section of this community – the increasingly isolated urban working class. And Marie Jones, especially in *A Night in November* has written from an explicitly Protestant, post-Ceasefire perspective. More relevantly to the present discussion, her slapstick musical reworking of a simpler earlier play, *Weddin's, Wee'ins and Wakes*, succeeded in presenting the celebratory and carnivalesque aspects of the Orange Marching season, without seeking to deny or apologize for its more sectarian associations. The exuberance of the performance appealed to a

broadly-based audience, and again comedy proved a fruitful medium for addressing ideas that seemed intractably complex and
difficult in the first instance.

Conventional critical response to *Caught Red Handed* was mixed,
with many of the local reviewers focussing on structural teething
problems, rather than the play's ideas. But the production
generated an unusually high level of response in the 'news' pages,
and featured in political reports on both television and radio. BBC
Radio 4's 'flagship' *Today Programme* used a recording of Dan
Gordon fulminating as 'The Leader' without introduction, which
at first hearing I assumed to be (as was clearly the intention) the
Reverend Ian Paisley. (The source was then back-referenced by the
journalist.) Extracts from the play were also used by BBC
Television's current affairs programme, *On the Record*, to frame a
report on Ulster Loyalism.

The unusual pattern of media coverage serves to demonstrate
both the play's efficacy as a catalyst for discussion, but also the
way in which its comic form might seem to undermine its artistic
credibility. The distinction between a critic and a reviewer is that
the former writes for posterity and the latter primarily for the
information of the potential current audience. By this definition,
most critical response to *Caught Red Handed* took the form of
'reviews'. Nevertheless, consciously or unconsciously, reviewers
still have at the backs of their minds the verdict of future
researchers and readers, and the benchmark by which most new
Irish plays are judged tends to involve the extent to which they can
be expected to become future classics.

Underpinning this process in a northern Irish context has been
a traditional critical disdain for farcical comedy, driven in part, I
believe, by the extent to which this has been synonymous with
indigenous Ulster Theatre. The long tradition of vernacular
comedy in Belfast emerged from the middle of the twentieth century, when the Group Theatre was a prolific producer of new
plays. By the late 1960s, the old Group with its broadly-based
repertoire had been supplanted by the work of James Young, and
the Group rejoiced in the title – 'The Home of Ulster Comedy'.
Even Young's popularity and resilience could not survive the full
onslaught of the Troubles in the early 1970s, however, and there is

a poignant echo of the Group's collapse in the press reports announcing the demise of Belfast's other leading theatre management, the Arts Theatre, shortly afterwards on 15 October, 1971 – their last desperate effort to stave off closure was a production of *The Love Nest* by the principal exponent of traditional 'Ulster Comedy', Sam Cree.

In the dark days that followed, the vernacular tradition of Ulster theatre was kept alive by the amateur companies, reinforcing its lack of respectability among exponents of serious drama. These plays, it seemed, were not destined for posterity as future classics. And yet, it was to be the very techniques these plays had marshalled in order to attract a large local audience to the theatre that were to serve first the record-breaking box office success of *We Do It For Love*, and later the phenomenon that was Charabanc. Plays that spoke to their audience in a familiar voice, and above all with a similar sense of humour, were to prove a powerful vehicle for the transmission of difficult ideas.

The expectation among critics and funders that the credibility of a new play depends on its potential to be a future classic is a pervasive one. The course of Irish theatre is marked by such signposts – *The Playboy of the Western World, The Hostage, Translations,* and above all O'Casey's Dublin trilogy. But was O'Casey really motivated, when he wrote these plays, by the lure of posthumous fame? Surely their contemporary power and lasting popularity are based precisely on the fact that they were written for the here-and-now – or should that be for the then-and-there? Modern commissioners of plays would, in my view, often serve their own interests better if they set their sights more on immediate concerns than the verdict of posterity.

The plays under consideration here are particularly perishable examples. *Caught Red Handed* explicitly invites this description through its not-too-distant futuristic setting. Since much of the point of the play depends on it taking place in 2005, it was clearly conceived with a limited shelf life in mind. This is no *1984* viewed from the distance of 1948. As for *We Do It For Love*, this too was a play responding to immediate needs, which despite its enormous success in 1975, proved to generate much less public interest when revived only two years later.

Does this lack of longevity make the drama itself less valid? I would argue not. Theatre that answers a particular need has huge value in addressing political stasis. As Christopher Murray observes in *Twentieth Century Irish Drama* (1997), the central image of *We Do It For Love* is a roundabout, pointing to the way in which people in Northern Ireland felt trapped in a cycle of violence. Charabanc spoke to a similarly closed mindset when they began to address gender politics in the following decade. And the loop from which Tim Loane's play seeks escape is the seemingly equally intractable round of peace negotiations. When there seems to be no way out, comedy provides a way of subverting the endlessness of the pattern.

In *We do It for Love* the cycle is broken symbolically (and literally) with the destruction of the play's central motif – a fairground roundabout. In *Caught Red Handed*, the sense of inevitability is challenged in the words Loane gives to Wayne, the son of the deceased leader:

> There is another way for us. There has to be … We might lose our flag … (*He rips the Union flag from the podium*) but no-one can crumple our culture. And let no-one tell you that Protestant culture is about how we fight or who we hate; it's about our reasoned voice of dissent … (Loane, 57)

These sentiments were dismissed as 'simplistic' and 'sugary' by Jim Wells, (the one member of Ian Paisley's party, the DUP, known to have attended the production) when he was interviewed for the BBC's *Stormont Live*. In the same programme, Arts Minister, Michael McGimpsey was much more positive. He was also quoted in a *Belfast Telegraph* feature on the production as saying that 'the play gave a light-hearted slant on unionism's passage from emotionalism to rationalism' – a remark that recalls Robin Glendinning's play, *Summerhouse*, where the stages of grief from anger to acceptance are used as a metaphor for the changing fortunes of unionism.

Perhaps the most incisive comment on *Stormont Live* came from Progressive Unionist Party leader, David Ervine (himself a descendant of the leading Ulster playwright of the first part of the last century, St. John Ervine), who welcomed the opportunity for political analysis 'through a wonderful and entertaining medium'. That such an array of politicians had all attended the play was in itself remarkable, albeit partly engineered by Tinderbox, who held a special political-guest night with a post-show discussion. The practical effect of this was to sidestep the arts pages, and secure the production a much wider publicity profile. Interestingly, when Tinderbox presented *Vote, Vote, Vote*, which featured a selection of short plays explicitly intended to reflect on the 2003 elections to the Northern Ireland Assembly, the press response was much more muted, suggesting that drama engages with politics best when it does not seek to play an overtly political game.

In order to capitalize on the populist potential of *Caught Red Handed*, but also with the honest intention of trying to reach what they perceived as a key working-class target audience for the play's ideas, Tinderbox organized a 'compass-points' community tour of Belfast in the Autumn of 2002. Linked to an outreach programme, and supported substantially through specialized 'diversity' funding, performances were given in the Golden Thread Theatre in North Belfast, the Tower Street Theatre in predominantly loyalist East Belfast, Amharclann na Carraige in nationalist West Belfast, and Queen's University's Elmwood Hall in South Belfast. At Queen's the play attracted a more traditional theatre audience with a higher-than-usual proportion of students, but in the north, west and east, the outreach work attracted less typical audiences with arguably less opportunity of 'detachment' (in Damian Gorman's sense) from violent politics.

Speaking at a post-show discussion after one of the performances at Queen's, Tim Loane reported that the community tour had been an enlightening experience. While working-class audiences on both 'sides' had been as reluctant as the first night audience publicly to vote for or against a United Ireland, Loane had a clear sense that his exposure of political hypocrisy was much less necessary in this context than he had expected. These performances brought home to him that while the middle-class of both traditions continue to be in denial, in working-class areas, *Caught Red Handed* was largely preaching its impatience and anger to the converted.

A similar argument could be made in relation to *We Do It For Love*, and for the more serious 'Troubles Dramas' that followed it onto the Lyric stage in the late 1970s and early 1980s. It is often the middle-class mainstream theatre audience that are most in need of comedic enlightenment.

These two plays, produced nearly thirty years apart, share a common stimulus – a sense of stasis. But the capacity of the political establishment directly to engage with this process in 2002 was one indication of how far things had changed across the decades, and offers a little hope that Belfast's failed bid for European City of Culture in 2008 was not perhaps as much an act of satire as it might at first have seemed.

Sources

Galvin, Patrick, *We Do It for Love* in *Three Plays*. Belfast: *Threshold*, Lyric Players Theatre, 1976 (*Threshold* No. 27).

Gebler, Carlo, Foreword to *One Belfast: Where Hope and History Rhyme (Belfast Bid for European Capital of Culture 2008)*. (Belfast: Imagine Belfast, 2001).

Gorman, Damian, *Devices of Detachment* (London: BBC Education, 1992).

Loane, Tim, *Caught Red Handed* (Belfast: Tinderbox Theatre Company, 2002).

Vote, Vote, Vote. (Belfast: Tinderbox Theatre Company, 2003).

5 | Turning The World Upside Down:
The Space Of Carnival and Playing The Fool in Frank McGuinness's *Innocence*
Anne F. O'Reilly

> I started to laugh because it hit me you were looking at them from above, so you must see them all upside-down, and I knew then somehow we'd won, we turned the world upside-down, the goat and the whore, the queer and the woman. *Innocence*

Innocence: The life and death of Michelangelo Merisi, Caravaggio by Frank McGuinness has had very few performances. The Gate production for the 1986 Irish Theatre Festival has been the only professional one (and even the in-house video has been lost). Some amateur companies have attempted it, (one in a pub), and in a conversation with McGuinness he mentioned a rumour of an off-Broadway production with David Bowie, which never materialized.

Ostensibly based on the real-life figure of the medieval painter Caravaggio, the play takes place over the course of one day in his life. The two acts (Life and Death) are almost superimposed one on the other, and take us into the reality of Caravaggio's life at conscious and unconscious levels. His creative and volatile personality (in real life he was accused of murdering a man) is captured in the movement of the play. The main characters are Caravaggio, his lover/friend Lena, the Cardinal (for whom Caravaggio works), and two younger homosexuals named Lucio and Antonio. Themes of patronage and prostitution alert the audience to the social and political reality of Caravaggio's world. The power of the medieval Church is very evident throughout the play. Carvaggio's ambivalent relationship with his own sexuality is mirrored in the behaviour of other characters, and also surfaces in the long dream sequence of the second act.

McGuinness recalls the newspaper headline from *The Evening Press* in 1986 which ran, 'Gay play shocks festival', and suggests that it is the content of the play that inhibits theatre companies from producing it. Whether that resistance is located in relation to the crude and overt references to homosexuality and the Catholic church or to the darkness of the artistic vision and journey that the protagonist undergoes, it is a play that deserves to be revisited. I would like to offer a vantage point for interpretation which is more aware of the play's potential as comedy than a cursory reading might suggest.

While there have been limited opportunities to experience an actual performance of the play, imagining what might be done by a director prior to a new performance is a worthwhile (and in-expensive) exercise. In this article, I offer a method of testing performance by offering some theoretical reflections and imagin-ative horizons that might help theatre practitioners in interpreting and staging this much neglected play.

The lens of carnival and the figure of the fool provide useful starting points for imagining a performance of this play. When we also consider carnival in the context of the medieval world, where it was often closely aligned with parody and rituals of reversal, it can provide an opening for an interpretation of Caravaggio as a lord of misrule, who turns the world upside down by his antics. The play in turn can then be seen as offering the audience a new vantage point for interpretation both of Caravaggio's world and our contemporary one.

Catherine Belsey has proposed the idea of theatre offering interrogative texts where the question of subjectivity is more fluid and the play is interpreted and presented in terms of a contest of meanings within culture. It seems appropriate to consider *Innocence* in such terms. It is also important to consider the play in terms that are not confined by the conventions of realism. It is a highly theatrical piece both in its imagery and its foregrounding of a carnivalized world. A familiarity with the paintings of Caravaggio adds additional colour to how one imagines both characters and props. Alfred Moir's introduction to the paintings and world of Caravaggio is particularly helpful. McGuinness in conversation drew my attention to the paintings of *John the Baptist*, *The Weeping Magdalen* and *The Death of the Virgin* as direct inspiration for the characters of Lucio, Lena and Anna. The red drape that figures in many of the paintings is a very important theatrical prop throughout the play.

Riana O'Dwyer writes of McGuinness's plays as dancing in the borderlands. This requires that we pay attention to the creation of liminal space within what Peter Brook has termed the 'empty space' of theatre. This liminal space is neither here nor there, more like a threshold (*limen*/threshold) between worlds, and is often invoked in discussions of carnival. From the opening tableau to the longer dream sequence of the second act, one must attempt theatrically to create a borderland space.

As audience we must be invited into the dreaming, murderous unconscious of Caravaggio. The depths of his darkness and despair may give us insight into his creativity, as we become aware of the awful complexities and compromises of the artist, forced into patronage and prostitution by the social conditions of his age. Caravaggio's madness is the madness of the outsider, the person forced to the periphery by the prevailing orthodoxy. From this vantage point he can be perceived as both dangerous and essential to the Church. The Cardinal who is Caravaggio's patron speaks of him as a 'disruptive servant' who lacks discretion. Nonetheless, he is needed for his 'whore's expertise' and is feared for being 'the painter of the poor' and reminding the hierarchy of 'unpleasant truths'.

But can we interpret the play as part of an Irish comic tradition? Vivian Mercier's analysis in *The Irish Comic Tradition* (1962) alerts us to its roots in an ancient tradition, steeped in magic, ritual and myth, and ranging from the fantastic to the macabre and grotesque. If we hold this broad interpretation of comedy then we can locate *Innocence* within it. The territory of the play is the ordinary and banal. This is no lofty space of transcendence but the grotty hovel or kip where Lena (prostitute and lover/friend to Caravaggio) lives in poverty. The ritual opening of the play pulls us down to earth, to the physical, the sexual, the animal. The temporarily blinded Caravaggio may proclaim his genius to Lena but she suggests alternative lines: 'I am Michelangelo Merisi and I am a wanker.' The physical sexual body subject to hunger, lust, sickness, disease, ageing and death is the inescapable reality. This grotesque body which, affected by mutability, could never enter the sublime is the baseline to which this play recalls us again and again.

The earthiness of humour that reconnects us with bodies, sexuality, hunger, disease and death is the same energy that is associated with the carnivalesque, where travesty and transgression enable transformation and renewal. The medieval experience of carnival had the overall effect of debasing or bringing down to earth. It allowed the sacred and the profane to become enmeshed rather than held apart as separate realms. The pattern of death and renewal in the mock crownings and de-crownings allowed a laughter at exalted objects which was at least ambivalent. Mikhail Bakhtin's study of carnival (*Rabelais and His World*) alerts us to how a festivalized degradation allowed a renewed contact with the earth as both womb and tomb. Similarly he notes how the reconnection with the grotesque body through the true feast of time which was carnival stood in sharp contrast to the official ecclesiastical celebrations of medieval times.

Simon Dentith's work on parody draws attention to many medieval examples of liturgical parody where the experience of carnival and the mockery of all that was held sacred allowed an experience of release from the crushing authoritarianism, intolerance, and intimidation of a hierarchical church. The Feast of Fools, celebrated on the Feast of the Holy Innocents on 28 December, allowed junior clergy to perform an elaborate parody of the church's liturgy, in which they elected a bishop or abbot of fools, dressed in women's clothes or vestments worn back to front, and engaged in various rituals of inversion which were often obscene or blasphemous. The feast heralded a space of undisciplined wildness, unrestrained wantonness and irresponsibility. Whether such ritual transgression merely maintained the status quo while containing dissent or whether it enabled genuine renewal is difficult to ascertain. Capturing the essence of this carnivalesque spirit in the theatre suggests a very physical approach, one that moves with energy and passion, and is not afraid of the frenzied excess that can accompany such celebration. The chaotic energy needs to be both explored and contained within the dramatic space.

Linda Henderson writes about the world of *Innocence* as a world of darkness, inhabited by creatures of the night. She interprets it as a world moved by primal and Dionysian forces of hunger, disease, lust, drunkenness, avarice, and violence, and sees it as a world dominated by Caravaggio as a lord of misrule. Caravaggio's behaviour seems to speak an alternative, disruptive language that breaks up received patterns of meaning and offers new interpretations. As Caravaggio immerses himself in the significance of the flesh, he becomes wilfully monstrous as he defies the symbolic order. The foregrounding of male homosexuality further questions his society's notion of compulsory heterosexuality. In turn, the religious vision of Caravaggio's paintings is scandalous in portraying the poor, the prostitute – those on the margins as manifestations of the divine. The question facing the practitioner is how to encourage an audience to glimpse this otherness.

The opening ritual prayer of the play 'Thou, O Lord, wilt ope my lips and my tongue shall announce Thy praise', transfers the traditional ritual to the new sacred space of theatre where the audience is invited to witness a new kind of miracle – where the artist (both as playwright and painter) will transform the stuff of everyday into the lasting beauty of art. The re-appropriation of prayer traditionally reserved for the sacred space of church, and the parody of sacred rites and blessings that occurs throughout the play, invite a new kind of imagining. Humorous exchanges, bawdy banter, and crude riposte break up the action of the play, questioning received assumptions and offering a counterpoint to the dominant thinking. The pace of the text might be embodied as fast, furious, the conversations punctuating its rhythm.

A street scene introduces the characters of Antonio and Lucio – male prostitutes, waiting to be hired. Their humorous exchange cannot hide the poverty and desperation of their situation ('A whore for the sake of your belly … Hunger drives you mad'). When Antonio and Lucio try the last resort (prayer) the following dialogue occurs:

Lucio: You pray.

Antonio: Hear us father in Heaven.

Lucio: We're hungry.

Antonio: We could eat each other.

Lucio: Not that. Say something religious.

Antonio: Such as?

Lucio: This is my body.

Antonio: This is my blood.

Lucio: Turn me into bread, God.

Antonio: Me into wine.

Lucio: Give us a miracle.

Antonio: Give us a man.

Lucio: Not even that. Work a reverse job. Flesh and blood into bread and wine.

Antonio: Give us a feed, Lord, if it's only ourselves.

(McGuinness,1996, p.222)

The two men appropriate the ritual words of the Eucharist, 'This is My Body/This is My Blood', as religious language to frame a desperate prayer for food. The parody and ritual reversal implied in the idea that they seek a reverse job, to be turned into bread and wine to feed each other may appear at one level sacrilegious or scandalous. At another it may in fact be a truer understanding of what the symbol of Eucharist implies – being changed or transformed in order to nurture one another in relationship. Awareness of the play of medieval parody may suggest ways that a scene like this might be played, with a kind of mock seriousness, that radically questions all assumptions.

Animal imagery which emerges early in the play brings an earthiness that combines both the magical and the grotesque. In the palace of the Cardinal, Caravaggio plays the fool and leads a carnival of the animals in a drunken night of frenzy and excess. The energy of carnival with its trust in the ridiculous and the illogical or inappropriate offers a site for transformation and renewal. The laughter of the carnival however is not simple parody. It combines both the comic and the tragic, becoming almost serious, an effect which Julia Kristeva notes in her understanding of carnival. In its seriousness it allows another perspective to emerge that questions all received interpretations.

This place of transgression and play allows the exploration of roles and identities while introducing themes of repression and transference. These might also be explored in pre-production workshops. The mock fight and transformation into animals both real and mythical pushes the play beyond the realist frame and enables a questioning of received images of subjectivity and sexuality. Lucio becomes a hound, a wild horse, a fire-breathing dragon and a bull. Antonio becomes in turn a hare, an eagle, and a fighting bull. Caravaggio becomes a poisonous lizard: 'Creeping on you. Touching you. Kissing you. Poison.' – an obvious reference to AIDS.

Caravaggio calms the two men, calling them his unicorns, while Lena had called Caravaggio a unicorn and a goat earlier in the scene. The animal imagery continues as Caravaggio and Lucio talk about scars and wounds. Both Caravaggio and Lucio were kicked by a horse and sustained wounds – Lucio on his thigh, Caravaggio a scar on his face. The wound on the thigh is possibly a castration which could also carry a wounding in the generative function – a wounding that runs through the play. Later Caravaggio will name and bless the animals in a chorus of transgression. In a final litany, he prays for the protection and preservation of the species. The prayer has pagan and deeper mythological undertones:

> Dragon, breathe your web of fire.
> Steed, open your trusty mouth.
> Bull, charge with a beating heart.
> Lizard, change colour for ever.
> Hare, lie with the sleeping hound.
> Eagle, see with all seeing eye.
> Hound, play with the wounded lion.
> Lion, roar your lament of love." (280)

And yet there are elements of the prophet Isaiah:

> The wolf shall dwell with the lamb,
> and the leopard shall lie down with the kid (Is. 11:6)

for whom the reversal of the established order can herald the dawning of a new age. The representation of the animals, whether through mime, shadow, mask, or puppet, stands to push the play beyond its realist frame and in turn highlight its theatricality.

Another important way of imagining this play in performance is to consider Caravaggio as playing the fool. The Cardinal refers to Caravaggio both as his animal and his fool. But as his fool he is on a leash and has no power in the Cardinal's house. The real transgressive and interruptive power of the fool however runs through the play. The character of Caravaggio embodies many aspects of the fool in his topsy-turvy representation of a world, his liminal status and his ability to journey to the depths of what it means to be human. From the wild trickster spirit to the wise or holy fool, however one imagines, casts or plays Caravaggio, the fool must enable both him and the other characters to celebrate a new wisdom, which is embodied and particular, and one that challenges the received orthodoxies about salvation and damnation.

In a wild, mad carnivalesque gesture Caravaggio tears the tapestries and paintings from the walls of the palace, as he ransacks the room and slashes the cushions. The others steal a bag of booty which includes a chalice, a gold cross, a silver bowl and a red cloak. The greed to possess life and literally to have more to eat and drink motivates the theft which is so often at the heart of comedy. The redistribution of the symbols of the church amongst the poor adds to the sense of the toppling of hierarchies so characteristic of medieval parody.

Lena has a dream in which she imagines herself in a beautiful room with all of Caravaggio's paintings, and she imagines that she can still see him in them even though he has gone. Suddenly she looks up and sees him looking down at her and says:

> ... I started to laugh because it hit me you were looking at them from above, so you must see them all upside-down, and I knew then somehow we'd won, we turned the world upside-down, the goat and the whore, the queer and the woman. (284)

Turning the world upside-down is the task of the fool. Following Caravaggio's own dream sequence in the second act the audience witnesses a descent into the unconscious (or dream consciousness) and an encounter with the dark. This descent opens to an otherness which foregrounds the interconnected issues of damnation, homosexuality, guilt and transgression. It is the traditional descent into Hell or Hades now represented by the individual's journey to the Self. Here the conscious mind drops into the archaic world of the unconscious as it journeys deeper into the dark.

Caravaggio becomes the holy fool, the wise fool who leads us through his own descent into his own darkness. It is a ritual enactment of a shamanic journey towards a retrieval of something that has been lost. The journey of soul retrieval is done on our behalf. Through this journey he meets with the damned, and those traditionally outside or on the margins of orthodoxy or respectability. In facing the depths of his own negativity, his capacity for self-destruction and annihilation, Caravaggio comes face to face with all who have been negatively defined – all who are other to the dominant naming. In a Christ-like fashion he descends into Hell, and prepares a space for creativity and living.

Caravaggio's journey through the dream sequence enables a deeper seeing to emerge. With its many reversals and mock benedictions the play continues in the parodic mode of medieval rituals. The more repressed a community is, the more extreme its rituals of reversal. Perhaps such rituals can become sources of empowerment to those traditionally marginalized or disempowered. The Cardinal (in role as Servant) utters a mock benediction that reverses the traditional belief system. He mocks salvation and in its place blesses the damned. His blessing concludes with a denial of God – 'There's nothing there' – and an invitation to Caravaggio to give up believing. Perhaps this is the truly mystical moment, the awareness of nothing, the emptiness at the centre. The medieval mystic Meister Eckhart prayed to God that he might rid him of God.

The characters of Lucio, Antonio and the Whore enter the dream sequence. They were Cararavaggio's models for his painting but he could not save them. They have died from drowning, disease and hunger and cry out for ritual burial. Caravaggio has fed off his models – they have been his bread and cheese but also his genius and his reputation. And while he has brought their lives to light in his paintings, they will still perish in darkness – at least in this historical time. As light streams from Caravaggio's raised hands he calls each of his models from the darkness. Caravaggio ritually moves to each of the characters, and dries the Whore's hand in his own, wipes the disease away from Antonio's face, kisses Lucio. The words of healing are poetic, ritualistic, incantatory. They call on the spirits in a ritually transgressive way. The drowned whore is asked to 'Pray for us sinners' in place of the Virgin Mary; the god of the grape, Bacchus, is invoked in praise and celebration of Lucio's body. Caravaggio dramatically calls the models from their frames as he stands in the fullness of his power as fiery shape-changing dragon painter that he is. One way of imagining the shape-changing Caravaggio and his models emerging from the paintings is to consider the use of projected images, where images from the play and from the original paintings could be superimposed, providing a useful visual dimension to the artist's world.

When Lena in the final moments of the play dresses Lucio like John the Baptist, in the props that were stolen from the palace, she is reproducing the creative impulse of Caravaggio. As she admires the beauty of her composition she calls on Caravaggio: 'Can you see us? It goes on and on.' She laughs – a laugh that the whole play has moved towards. The play ends with music, light and the sound of Caravaggio's laughter. This is not polite laughter but visceral laughter that comes from the bowels of the earth itself. This is the laughter of the trickster spirit, the spirit of disorder and enemy of boundaries and definitions. This is the laughter that recreates the world. The survival of the paintings and the impulse towards creativity is like the cosmic joke – the final laugh of something greater that survives.

Sources

Bakhtin, Mikhail, *Rabelais and His World,* trans. Hélène Iswolsky (Bloomington: Indiana University Press, 1984).

Dentith, Simon, *Parody* (London: Routledge, 2000).

Henderson, Linda, 'Innocence and Experience', *Fortnight* CCXLV, Nov. 1986.

Jordan, Eamonn, *The Feast of Famine* (Bern: Peter Lang, 1997).

Kristeva, Julia, 'Word, Dialogue and Novel', in *The Kristeva Reader*, ed. Toril Moi (Oxford: Blackwell, 1986).

McGuinness, Frank, 'Innocence: The life and death of Michelangelo Merisi, Caravaggio' in *Frank McGuinness: Plays 1* (London: Faber and Faber, 1996).

McGuinness, Frank, in conversation with Anne F. O'Reilly, Dublin, 2002.

Mercier, Vivian, *The Irish Comic Tradition* (Oxford: Oxford University Press, 1962).

Mirami, Hiroko, *Frank McGuinness and his Theatre of Paradox*, Ulster Editions and Monographs, 12 (Buckinghamshire: Colin Smythe, 2002).

Moir, Alfred, *Caravaggio* (London: Thames and Hudson, 1989).

O'Dwyer, Riana, 'Dancing in the Borderlands: The plays of Frank McGuinness', in *The Crows behind the Plough: History and Violence in Anglo-Irish Poetry and Drama*, ed. Geert Lernout (Amsterdam, Atlanta: Rodopi, 1991).

Vice, Sue, *Introducing Bakhtin* (Manchester: Manchester University Press, 1997).

6 | Comedy in Fishamble plays
Jim Culleton

Fishamble has produced very little that you might call pure 'comedy', although most playwrights who have written for us have used comedy in their work for various reasons. When I was directing each of the plays explored in this essay, I was fascinated by the variety of reasons for the use of comedy and how it worked with an audience. When the plays were performed, the comic effect of a scene depended on the writing itself, obviously, but also on the rapport created between the actors and audience. In fact, it seems to me that it should be difficult – if comedy really works in performance – to differentiate between the comic writing itself and the skill of the actors who, with timing and honesty, convey the comedy of a situation to the audience. This essay is an attempt to explore how comedy is used – and how it can work in performance – in a half dozen plays written for the company over the past seven years. It includes insights taken from conversations with the playwrights involved.

Comedy is tragedy interrupted   (Alan Ayckbourn)

Many of Ireland's most celebrated playwrights, like Beckett and O'Casey, have revelled in creating laughter in darkness, finding fun in the pain and torture of living. In their comedy, laughter is never very far from tears. Much of contemporary Irish writing for the theatre seems to work in this tradition of using comedy to explore the darker side of human experience. This is certainly true in some of the plays written for Fishamble, including *Red Roses and Petrol*

(1995) by Joe O'Connor, which was produced under our original name, Pigsback.

Joe points to the closeness of comedy to painful human experience, noting the amount of pain and destruction that is involved in the language we use for laughter:

> We speak of roaring with laughter, side-splitting, screaming, crying, howling, slapping backs, punch-lines, fall-guys. 'I laughed till I cried – till I thought I was going to die.' When we laugh, the face contorts. The eyes water. Laughter comes from the same emotional place as grief, or longing, or perhaps even sex. It is one of the few moments in everyday life when we lose control over what we are doing. Many dramatists and storytellers have understood the potential of that moment to throw the audience off guard; the better to hit them with the serious stuff.

To my mind, the humour in *Red Roses and Petrol* often came from the incongruity of seemingly unlinked events being juxtaposed. Joe agreed that the fun often comes from the yoking together of disparate elements by violence: 'A man in a dress. A bucket of water in the face. A corpse sits up and comes back to life. Things which are not supposed to happen are often the funniest,' Joe suggests. *Red Roses and Petrol* features a scene, which audiences seemed to find funny, in which a widow, Moya, divides up the ashes of her late husband, Enda, into tupperware lunchboxes:

> **Medbh:** Which one's mine?
> **Moya**: (*Pointing*) That one.
> **Medbh:** How come you're giving her more than me? Gimme a bit more.
> **Moya:** Would you have a bit of respect, for God's sake.
> **Medbh** (*Fighting back laughter*) Sorry, Ma.
> *Moya continues the delicate operation.*
> **Medbh:** Can I lick the spoon?
> **Moya:** Medbh Doyle, I'll skelp you in a minute.
> **Catherine:** Well, I don't care. I'm not bringing daddy back to New York in a lunch box.

Joe recalls:

> Later, Moya's son, a user of cocaine, mistakenly snorts his father's ashes, thinking them profoundly Columbian in origin. I remember

once having a conversation with the actor who played the part, where he wondered what it meant to inhale your da. I didn't really know what to say. It must have meant something, but I don't know what. Or perhaps it means nothing other than the grotesquerie it is; a ridiculous moment where a taboo is broken. Perhaps those are the moments where humour is to be found.

This was an exciting moment in performance, as audience reactions were usually an edgy mixture of laughter, shock and outrage. At another point in the play, Medbh talks about her father in the coffin, with his hair combed to the wrong side, 'across his head, to make him look like he wasn't bald. He looked like Jackie fucking Charlton lying in the coffin. It was terrible'. The moment relies on finding fun in something so potentially upsetting. When rehearsing comedy in a play, the humour can often cease to be funny to those involved after a few weeks' rehearsal, but Joe's humour is placed so carefully on a knife-edge that it never happened with this play.

The comedy is black too, and full of startling juxtapositions, in the work of Mark O'Rowe. He also explores taboo subjects, often shocking audiences with his mixture of seediness and hilarity. When Fishamble produced *From Both Hips* (1997), audiences were impressed by the way Mark always maintained a dark threat of violence under a veneer of comic invention. There were many performances at which the audience seemed appalled because it had laughed at something that later transpired to be either repulsive, abusive or both. The comedy is certainly warped and perverse and, I think, all the funnier for it. This play is both hilarious and disturbing, combining farcical comedy with a look at violation on many levels. While the play has a volatile, spontaneous feel, some of the comedy works in a very traditionally, well-structured way. I remember vividly rehearsing a scene between Marion O'Dwyer (Liz) and Fionnuala Murphy (Theresa). Theresa loves her dog and has begun to smell of him; Liz has read an article about how dogs are not capable of love; Liz decides to tell Theresa about her discovery. However, Theresa is having an affair with the husband of Liz' sister, Adele, and thinks Liz is referring to *him* not loving her:

Theresa: (*Thinking she's been rumbled*) How did you know?
Liz: Know what?
Theresa: Know about us? How come you knew?
Liz: I can smell him off you. Sometimes you've got hairs on you.
What do you mean?
Theresa (*Confused*) Hairs?
Liz: His hairs.
Theresa: I ... (*Pause*)
Liz: It's all right. C'mere. Do you want a hug? Come over here.
Theresa: No, I'm all right.
Liz: You don't look all right. Sometimes a hug...
Theresa: No. No. The ... (*Pause*) You can smell him off me?
Liz: Not bad. It's nothing you have to be embarrassed about.
(*Pause*)
Theresa: I feel like a gobshite.

The situation is wonderful and full of comic misunderstandings, mistaken identities and double meanings. In rehearsals, we had to remind ourselves that the characters could not acknowledge the humour in the scene as they both believe they are talking about the same traumatic discovery. Audiences really seemed to enjoy their 'inside knowledge' of the misunderstanding and seeing how it resolved itself. I talked to Mark about the sense of danger underneath his warped comedy and about using traditional structures to create comedy in this play. He remarked that he is not aware of using any formal structures, even though he admires writers who can consciously include a gag or a humourous section in a play:

I've never written a completely serious play, I just can't help myself. But you're right to say that the humour is warped. I sometimes find that what I write is hilarious to me but that no-one else finds it funny. That's fine, though, because the humour is often dark and scary. So if people laugh, that's fine; if not, that's fine too – it should work either way. The territory *From Both Hips* inhabits means that the comedy is undercut by danger and embarrassment, so it should be uncomfortable to laugh at it. A lot depends on the mood of a particular audience. I remember talking to an actor who was frustrated at the lack of audience response one night to the comic elements in the play. Perhaps an actor feels the need for laughter in this situation, but I'm happy whether people laugh at my humour or feel repulsed by it.

'Life is a tragedy when seen in close-up, but a comedy in long shot' (Charlie Chaplin)

In *Red Roses and Petrol* and *From Both Hips*, it seems that a perspective is given that allows us to laugh at events that are painfully unfunny when the laughter dies away. Perhaps this kind of laughter allows the audience to release tension and become more receptive to the pain behind it. Mark is interested in how comedy can work in this way. He reminded me of the moment at the end of *From Both Hips* when:

> Adele is in dire straits and the audience feels embarrassed and upset for her. Then Paul insults her, or makes a funny comment; the audience laughs and then feels bad for having laughed with him. But I don't think this laughter should let the audience off the hook; it should incriminate people in the audience and make them question the way that their laughter strengthened their link with the scummiest of characters.

It is one of the exciting elements of live theatre that every audience reacts differently. Laughter does not necessarily come in the same place each night. Laughter which comes at a dark moment in a play can be invigorating. Sometimes this is because an audience is concerned for a character and laughs nervously. I wonder though, with comedy and tragedy so closely linked, is there ever a danger of inappropriate laughter, or comedy working against a desire to have serious subject matter treated with respect by an audience. Joe remarked that, being something of a part-time theatre-writer, one from the background of the novel and the short story, it has often seemed to him that the audience, and not the actors, are in charge of the show. That a certain tyranny of laughter is sometimes in evidence and that sometimes it can murder whatever is happening on the stage:

> Comedy can sometimes be used to enter into a kind of unspoken contract of anesthesia. I'll inject you if you inject me. Yes, the theatre should be a good night out; but in an ideal world, it should be many other things too. Laughter is an extremely important weapon to have in your arsenal, but the more sparing the use, the deeper the effect.

Gavin Kostick also uses a lethal mixture of comedy and serious drama, but with a different objective to Joe or Mark in *The Flesh Addict* (1996). He is exploring the comedy of unease, looking at paranoia and violence in the world of the Pre-Raphaelite artists. But Gavin is anxious not to sugar the pill by using comedy to access more serious moments:

> The usual comedic progression is to create comedy which then gives way to serious or tragic moments. I wanted to reverse this by creating serious drama which was then undercut by humour, in the same way as the Pre-Raphaelites were dedicated to creating high art about serious subjects but were always struggling with the ludicrous nature of the world around them. So, when Rossetti states, 'I have created one undisputed masterpiece, and that is one more than Leonardo da Vinci ever did', his sense of achievement is undercut by the final, surreally comic sequence. When our first production of the play was on, some people felt I had not allowed emotions to emerge fully because I undercut serious dilemmas with spiteful comedy. After the burial of Lizzie Siddall, for instance, the Vicar loses his place in the funeral service; when William and Janey Morris are trying to have a family meal, their attempt is thwarted by everyone else in the room – apart from themselves – having a highly physical, sexual relationship; or when Rossetti realises his yellow paint changes colour on the canvas over time, he calls the paint manufacturer, Mr. Newton, in and conveys his horror and disgust to him:

Rossetti: All my yellows, for five years. I painted health. You have caused me sickness.

Newton: We are always seeking ways to improve our product.

Rossetti: How much further will it go?

Newton: I do not know.

Rossetti: You cur.

Newton: Mr Rossetti?

Rossetti: You cur. You dog, you disease, you jaundice.

Newton: No sir, this is ...

Rossetti: 'No sir'! 'No sir'. Will you 'no sir' me?

*Rossetti leaps upon **Newton**, and forces his mouth open. He squeezes the paint into him.*

Rossetti: I am Dante Gabriel Rossetti who intends to be the foremost artist of this or any other century and Rossetti will not be thwarted by the incompetence of merchants. Every time you shit I

want you to recall my lovely yellow that you have turned to shit.
Make me fixed colours. Fixed colours!

The comedy arising from Rossetti's frustration is quite cruel
and slapstick in nature. In performance, Robert Price portrayed
Rossetti as an obsessive, manic and almost deranged figure, so the
humour was a startling one, with a sense of menace never very far
away. Although the play deals with a specific group of artists, it
captures a universal predicament by showing how human en-
deavour and desire can be undermined by humour. Gavin feels
there is something faintly ludicrous about solemn moments, which
he wanted to release:

> Comedy is something you cannot avoid, sometimes. It leaks into
> serious human experience. When a person makes love for the first
> time, or gets married or is at a funeral, or whatever, the comedic
> element is very often present. This can sometimes be a healthy way
> of relieving tension or coping with major events, but it can also be
> destructive in that it can refuse people the right to be sincere, to
> experience profound emotions.

'It is only one step from the sublime to the ridiculous'

(Napoleon Bonaparte)

When Ian Kilroy wrote *The Carnival King* (2001) for Fishamble, he
explored profound emotions, in particular the resentment and
frustration experienced by the family of a murdered woman. The
murder is unsolved, although everyone in the area knows un-
officially who committed it. Ian investigated this dilemma by
writing a play which is a dark, grotesque farce set at carnival time.
This highlighted the ridiculous situation of the main protagonists
and created a tension between serious themes and their anarchic,
comic treatment. When I asked Ian why he had chosen to explore
such serious issues in a sometimes farcical way, he referred to
Patrick Kavanagh's comment in *Lough Derg* that it is the true Irish
spirit to joke through the Death-mask. 'What, you could ask, is
more serious than death? What a release, then, to laugh at it?' says
Ian:

> Sending up the serious is so basically human and is as old as human
> culture itself. To make light of what is grave is not only life
> affirming, but is essential to our survival. That is why each human

civilization has a version of the festive, a time for holding up death and laughing in its face. It allows us to momentarily escape from our dark fate in a gloriously subversive act of celebration. The Carnival King is informed by this impulse. While conscious of a society bereft of justice, it nevertheless seeks to offer a kind of psychic release, by laughing at and sending up the agents of injustice.

One such moment occurs, just after Sergeant Courtney has left Christy and Phillis. Christy (the brother of the murdered woman) and Phillis (who works for the local blood-bank) are frustrated by Courtney's ineptitude:

> **Phillis:** That fellow could do with being taken down a peg or two.
> **Christy:** Thinks he's a Lord, or something.
> **Phillis:** Yes…and he has the most common type of blood, you know.
> **Christy:** 'Would have been promoted years ago but for all his cock-ups.
> **Phillis:** You know the joke going round is the only good arrest he made was of young Joe Hennelly, and that was for his own suicide. *Christy and Phillis laugh.*
> **Phillis:** God forgive me, I shouldn't be saying that.
> **Christy:** God rest poor Joe Hennelly.

Comedy is used here to deal with uncomfortable subject matter. In performance, we were excited by the audience response which sometimes involved an uneasiness caused by the comic treatment of serious, upsetting subject matter. It also raised issues about whether comedy is really an appropriate medium through which to explore taboo subjects and whether there is any subject matter that should not be joked about. Ian feels comedy has always been used to explore taboo subjects:

> because it is only when the audience is laughing that it can be presented with subjects that it normally finds unpalatable. Through the transformative power of laughter, what is normally left unspoken can be revealed and examined in the light of day. The licence of laughter offers us a free space to interrogate all our taboos. The anarchic nature of comedy means that there is no situation that cannot be laughed at. What is essential is the role of the audience. We can laugh at the misfortune of others, but it is more difficult to laugh when that misfortune is closer to home. The

passage of time or distance in space is important to take into consideration when making a joke. In 2002, Irish American comedians can joke about the Potato Famine; they couldn't as easily in 1847. Similarly, the anonymous creators of street jokes in London can poke fun at the fall of New York's Twin Towers, but not as easily on the streets of New York itself. There are no taboos that should not be laughed at. The only thing is for the joker to judge well his or her audience.

Maeve Binchy and Jim O'Hanlon certainly judge their audiences well, though they are not using comedy to deal with quite such uncomfortable subject matter. Through comedy, they are exposing human foibles, commenting on the way society works, and laughing at the ridiculous situations in which characters find themselves. In *Wired to the Moon* (2001), Maeve Binchy exposes – with marvellously comic results – the insecurities of her characters. They include an agony aunt who has more problems than any of her correspondents, a woman who nearly has a nervous breakdown after inviting people around 'for something simple that is going to be no trouble', and a teacher who is fed up solving everyone else's problems:

> **Annie:** And the same in the staffroom. Never a problem of my own – always someone else's. (*To Miss O'Brien*) 'I know, I know, Miss O'Brien, it is very hard, of course it is, but you know, I get a feeling that Mr. Piazza would be more upset than relieved if you arrived at his house and told his wife Everything. Oh, I do see your point about total honesty, but Mr. Piazza might have thought of that one evening as something more ... well, not so much casual ... but something lovely, just to happen once, to be a beautiful memory. It would change from being a beautiful memory into being a Problem if you were to tell Mrs. Piazza about his having said he had loved you for years. No, don't cry, Miss O'Brien, please. I'm sure he did, and does, love you, but there are different degrees of love – especially to an Italian music master. I think his love for you is more the admiring-you-as-you-take-the-girls-out-to-hockey kind of love, than the leaving-his-wife-and-seven-children-and-renting-a-small-room-with-you sort.' (*To audience*) When would I have a problem of my own?

Maeve succeeds in creating wonderfully comic situations and releasing the laughter of recognition in an audience by sharing her insight into common predicaments with complete honesty and warmth. She says:

> Because I was always a fat girl, I learned early in life the art of self-deprecation and never taking yourself seriously. I always took my work seriously, but never myself. During many years of writing, I learned that what readers and audiences loved was to see a situation, a humbling embarrassing situation, which they can recognise, having been through it themselves. The single most popular article I ever wrote in The Irish Times was when I admitted that when I was 18, I didn't know whether you made your own bed in a hotel or not. Hundreds of people out there had the same problem and some of them still had it. Often the admitting of inadequacies in a comedy can create what begins by a nervous laugh, but turns into a wonderful, therapeutic laugh of relief. I am not the ONLY person in the world who drank a little bowl of water on a posh table instead of washing my fingers in it. How very liberating and wonderful! There's not much comedy in looking at people who are perfect and do everything right. That's more sick-making really.

Maeve very cleverly allows her audience in on the joke, so that the viewer can identify the mistake a character is about to make and then enjoy the resolution of the error. These moments (such as that when the Agony Aunt does not realize she knows the person to whom she is giving advice, but the audience does) worked very well with audiences relishing their implication in the intrigue. In performance, the comedy came from the truthfulness with which the situations were presented.

'We participate in a tragedy; at a comedy we only look'

(Aldous Huxley)

In *The Buddhist of Castleknock* (2002), Jim O'Hanlon also uses comedy to highlight the shortcomings, absurdities and incongruities of human behaviour. He delves into the psyche of a 'typical' Irish family gathered together for Christmas, with hilarious results, exposing fears and prejudices that lie just under the surface of his characters. I asked Jim if he agreed with Aldous Huxley's comment and whether he felt that powerful comedy had the potential to challenge and change an audience. He found it astonishing the notion that comedy can't be profound, or is always inherently *light* in some way. On the contrary, he says, 'comedy is a wonderful means of holding a mirror up to our own lives, of giving an audience the distance which, if you like, dupes that audience into thinking that it is laughing at someone else when in fact it is simply looking in a very cleverly constructed, and cunningly disguised, mirror. Laughing at a dramatic situation or at a set of characters does give us a certain distance, as Aldous Huxley suggests. But as Brecht said, it's those on the outside who are best placed to see the truth.' We discussed how, in the work of Molière, Beckett, much of Synge, O'Casey, even *Fawlty Towers,* the genius is in making us *think* we are on the outside looking in, when in fact it is our own lives which are under scrutiny. Sean O'Casey said:

> Laughter is brought in to mock at things as they are so that they may topple down, and make room for better things to come.

Jim puts the open-mindedness of a seemingly liberal middle-class family to the test when one of the grown-up children reveals he has converted to Buddhism, so will not be attending Christmas Mass, eating meat or drinking alcohol at Christmas dinner. Traditional family rituals and superstitions are reassessed through the consequences of this revelation. Jim uses comedy as a way into the world of the Irish family, as a means of dissecting the various tensions which often lurk beneath the apparent bonhomie. Prejudices bubble under the surface, for instance, as Edie and Sean discuss Rai, their son's black, English girlfriend, whom they have just met for the first time:

> **Sean:** Of course I like her. (*A beat*) Why, don't you like her?
> **Edie:** She seems like a lovely girl.
> **Sean:** There you are then. (*A beat*) Still and all – she's certainly ... how can I put it ... She's certainly more, well...tanned, than I expected.
> **Edie:** Sean!
> **Sean:** I'm not saying there's anything wrong with that. On the contrary, I think it's quite ... exciting. But there's no point in pretending we haven't noticed.
> **Edie:** It doesn't bother you?
> **Sean:** Not in the least. You?
> **Edie:** Good Lord, no.
> **Sean:** Great. I thought you might be ...

Edie: Well I'm not.

Comedy might give a sense of perspective which, in turn, provides a certain freedom for the playwright to explore areas of concern. I discussed with Jim whether comedy is ultimately less probing or hard-hitting than more serious drama. We agreed that comedy can be used sometimes as a cop-out, a means of making difficult or unpleasant truths more palatable for an audience. But comedy, when it's well-executed, can act as a very powerful tool for drawing people into a story or situation, for creating a world on stage which the audience wants to inhabit, wants to know more about, wants to experience. Jim felt that it's not a question of comedy providing the sugar which helps the medicine go down, but of it being just one device among many to draw us into the world of the story, the world of the characters. 'The best comedy,' it seems to him, 'is anything but light, or saccharine, or frivolous. On the contrary, it's driven by tremendous passion, and by a fierce desire to manage that passion and to express it. Anger, disappointment, sadness – the best comedy uses laughter as a means of confronting those emotions and expressing them. In some ways, the audience could be said to be hoodwinked into looking at some deeper, often unpleasant issues by clever use of comedy in a play. They're lulled into a false sense of security by the laughter, and then you can hit them with the sucker punch.'

The journey for many of the characters in *Wired to the Moon* is to realize that some of life's dilemmas are not as bad as they had previously imagined. This is conveyed with great comedy that allows for very powerful and incisive moments of epiphany in the play. *The Buddhist of Castleknock* uses comedy to say something quite specific and probing about the often subtle nature of racism. The characters realize they have been forgetting their priorities through the arguments of the play. There is a lot of fun and comic mayhem in these arguments that then gives way to the very startling confrontation of prejudices. It is possibly through the comedy of these plays that characters – and audiences – can be cajoled towards a thoughtful, and potentially unnerving, exploration of their behaviour.

'Whatever is funny is subversive'   (George Orwell)

Gavin Kostick feels comedy can be ultimately a conservative art form, where usually – through a series of encounters and mis-adventures – characters try to change themselves or their circumstances, only to realize that they were better off as they were. 'Some comedy is subversive, of course,' he suggests:

> If you think of Oscar Wilde's writing which destabilises the status quo and shows the way things are to be ridiculous. Or The Marriage of Figaro, for instance, in which all the funny lines are given to the servants, in order to laugh at the higher orders. Or in the literature of countries which are colonised or ruled by dictators, where comedy is used to mock the rulers and feel humanity in the face of oppression. More often than not, though, humour generates chaos, with relationships inverted and confused, but with the author reasserting basic decency and the advantages of staying within the social order, ultimately. If you think of *A Midsummer Night's Dream*, or any classical comedy, this is how it works.

Whether a comedy asserts or undermines the status quo depends on the intentions of the playwright and how successfully they are realized. In directing all the plays discussed here, it seemed that each play has a comedic element, but that laughter is sought for different reasons; each writer uses comedy to achieve similar overall goals, but also has a unique aim in incorporating comedy into the work. All the playwrights use comedy to entertain audiences and to capture what is ridiculous or amusing about human experience. Each writer also wants to have a specific effect on an audience through comedy. Joe O'Connor captures the pain in laughter, twisting the knife with his barbed wit; Mark O'Rowe uses comedy to create an uncomfortable sense of danger and warped violence; Gavin Kostick shows how serious human expression and achievement can be undermined and thwarted by comedy; Ian Kilroy explores the dark laughter of survival in the face of tragedy; Maeve Binchy shares the laughter of recognition and release with her audience; Jim O'Hanlon uses comedy to draw an audience into an analysis of its own foibles and attitudes.

In the production of the plays discussed, humour came most often from situations which were created with honesty in both the writing and performing. The most effective comedy often involved apparent opposites being connected in a way that was startling. Thanks to all the writers, actors and audiences who have created these memorable comic moments in order to explore dark and dangerous topics, make insightful observations on life and provide a unique view of the world in which we live.

Sources

Red Roses and Petrol, *From Both Hips* and *The Carnival King* are published in the Fishamble/Pigsback: *First Plays Anthology* (Dublin: New Island Books, 2002).

7 | An Irish Joke, a Nigerian Laughter
Olabisi Adigun

It is very true that the only constant thing in life is change. I think I have changed a great deal since the first time I arrived on these shores eight years ago. I speak, think, dress, behave and work differently. More importantly however, I have noticed that these days I laugh a lot. This, in my opinion, can be attributed to the fact that I (a foreigner) am, at last, 'getting' Irish jokes. Now I am confident that when I hear a good Irish joke, it is not only that I find it funny enough to laugh at, I also effortlessly understand its cultural context. And more than any requirement, the ability to understand a particular culture and its jokes is what is needed to enjoy that culture's theatrical presentations, especially comedy. Recently and probably for the very first time, I had the best laugh of my life as a non-Irish audience member watching an Irish play. It was the award-winning production of *A Night in November* written by Marie Jones and starring Marty Maguire as the solo actor. I will never forget that evening. Are you wondering why being able to laugh heartily watching an Irish comedy is such a big deal to me?

I am originally from Nigeria, a country I left for England in search of a greener pasture in 1993. Three years later, I arrived in Ireland and I have since made it my new home. I have been a lover of the theatre since childhood, so naturally I was curious about Irish theatre upon my arrival. To date, I have seen a variety of Irish plays. These include comedy, tragedy, melodrama, musicals, and dance drama. Out of all the Irish plays I have seen however, it is those labelled 'comedy' that were most difficult for me to understand or enjoy. On many occasions, I had been the only one in the audience who was not laughing, simply because I did not 'get' the joke. This, unarguably, can be attributed to the fact that I was not Irish and, as such, I had a lot to learn about Irish culture before I would be able to understand the nuances of Irish jokes – a main ingredient of Irish comedy. So the question is, what has changed, or what was different about *A Night in November*, that I found it so funny I laughed non-stop that fateful May evening? To answer this question, I would like to begin from the beginning.

I recall my first experience of seeing a 'typical' Irish play, which was less than a year after my arrival in Ireland. It was a production of Tom Murphy's *Bailegangaire* somewhere in Galway City. Ironically, the title of this play literally translates as 'a town without laughter'. Unsurprisingly, it was very bleak, but somehow, some moments in it still managed to generate laughter amongst the audience, a majority of whom were undoubtedly Irish. As for me, I remember that I found the play extremely difficult to understand. What also made the experience even more frustrating was the fact that I could not join in the few times the audience laughed when something funny was said. Because of this experience, it took me another three years to summon the courage to go to another Irish play.

This time it was Druid Theatre Company's production of *The Beauty Queen of Leenane* at the Gaiety Theatre here in Dublin. I went to see the production because it had gotten rave reviews when it was staged in the United States. My thinking was that if it could appeal to Americans, it should not be all that difficult for a non-Irishman like me to understand. To a large extent I was correct. In the first place, I could easily follow the plot of the play; and secondly and more importantly, I had been in Ireland long enough to recognize some of the resonances of Irish culture. So this experience, unlike the first, was not as excruciating. Nevertheless, one thing that I found deeply unsettling was what most people in the audience found really funny about the play. Most of the time when the audience laughed, it was when something funny was said or done at the expense of the powerless, senile old woman, who is trying desperately to hang on to her daughter, who should have been married a long time ago.

In my opinion so much laughter was generated that evening because most people in the audience could relate to the comic action unfolding on stage on all kinds of cultural and/or social levels. I, on the other hand, found it extremely difficult to partake in laughing at a helpless old woman, not simply because I am not Irish, but because in my culture – the *Yoruba* culture of Western Nigeria – such an act is considered taboo. We strongly believe that age is wisdom and as such it is disrespectful to laugh at the aged. In a sense, therefore, in order to laugh at jokes, we do not only have to 'get' them but we have to approve their emotions. This cultural notion of approving a joke seems to me to be what Umberto Eco asserts in his observation, 'The comic ... seems bound to its time, society, cultural anthropology', in his essay, 'The Comic and the Rule'. One can therefore argue that though we all laugh the same way, the kinds of things that are considered funny or make people laugh differs from one culture to the other. In other words what an Irish person would find very laughable because of its obvious acceptance within Irish society could be completely frowned upon by say, Nigerians.

Take farting as a typical example. On many occasions, I have had the misfortune to be around people who find farting openly really funny. And for some strange reason, this 'joke' never fails to generate laughter amongst Irish lads. In my culture farting intentionally is deemed disrespectful and as such is not considered funny. On the other hand it does generate laughter when its perpetrator cannot control him or herself. So in a way the laughter that accompanies the act of farting amongst the *Yoruba* people is to allay the victim's fear of being rebuked and to assure him/her, 'Don't worry we understand you couldn't control yourself'.

The act of drunkenness is another example that readily comes to mind. Although it is a sure way of generating laughter, and this has been exploited in all shapes or forms for dramatic purposes, I want to argue that, like farting, the way Irish people laugh at drunkenness is different from the way Nigerians laugh at it. In Nigeria, it is considered antisocial to be seen staggering drunkenly home after a night out. Here in Ireland, such a sight is very common and it is puzzling that it has never failed to generate laughter off and especially onstage. I have often wondered what is it that

Irish people find funny about someone who has spent his/her hard-earned money on getting 'legless'. Now that I have lived in Ireland for a while and have also had the opportunity to see a variety of artistic representations of its culture, I have come to the con-clusion that laughter of this nature, especially in the theatre, is what Sigmund Freud refers to as 'the laughter of unease'.

In his insightful essay titled, 'The Joy of Sex and Laughter', writer and psychoanalyst Adam Phillips describes jokes as our 'rather ingenious ways of getting pleasure from things we find un-acceptable'. Of late, the prevailing excessive drinking culture in Ireland seems to be attracting attention more than ever. All hands seem to be on deck to combat this societal malaise. While reasonable time is allocated to debate the issue in the grounds of the Dail chambers, the media, through various radio and television pro-grammes and newspaper articles is also contributing its quota to the campaign against unnecessary drunkenness. So far, as an art form and cultural antenna, the theatre's strategy, in my opinion, has been to present this sensitive issue, in such a way that more and more laughter is generated by it. 'As long as we laugh', Phillips argues, 'we are OK'. In other words, rather than being ashamed, embarrassed, sad or grief-stricken by something, we laugh at it. I remember vividly now the delirious laughter that accompanied the line, 'He was so drunk, he couldn't remember the second line to "Ole Ole ole ole" ', perfectly delivered in *A Night in November.* I myself laughed, especially because I know of people who had gotten so drunk that they had forgotten their names.

Now do not get me wrong. I am not by any means saying there are no good Irish jokes. Irish people, all over the world, are known for their 'gift of the gab' and good sense of humour. In fact, I believe that, in the way proverbs in African culture are invaluable to the art of conversation, so are jokes in Irish culture. I remember that, 'It is a joke', is the phrase that was regularly whispered to-wards my direction by my few Irish friends during my early days in Ireland when they felt that my Nigerian origin could stand in my way of enjoying a joke. How right they were. I was so clueless that I took it literally when I was told by someone the first time I visited Limerick, to count my fingers anytime I shook someone's hand. It is hard to believe now, but I actually did count my fingers as advised and it took me a couple of years to realize that it was a joke. This is, however, very ironic because, if I do say so myself, I was renowned for my sense of humour back home in Nigeria. But since I moved to Ireland, it is not only that I am no longer funny, I am also not always culturally equipped to see the funny side of a good Irish joke. But according to a Yoruba proverb, 'A corpse that has been buried for three months is no more a stranger in the graveyard'.

Having lived in Ireland for eight years, and been married to an Irish woman (with a good sense of humour) for four years, I hardly need any prompting to recognize, understand and laugh at a good Irish joke whenever I hear or see one. Take for instance the famous Roy Keane T-shirt I bought a few years ago. I was doing my last-minute Christmas shopping when I sighted this T-shirt on Dublin's Henry Street. The inscription in front of the T-shirt is divided into three parts, and it reads – at the top: *Roy Keane's Apology in Japanese*; in the middle are four Japanese-like words; and at the bottom is: *If you don't read Japanese tilt your head to the right.* When one tilts one's head to the right, the lettering in the middle, which initially appears like Japanese words, becomes decipherable English words, reading: *Go Fuck Yourself.* Personally, I found the T-shirt very funny and even more so when I discovered that the characters in the middle are truly Japanese letters (except that on this occasion they mean nothing in Japanese). It is a clever joke geared toward those people who lived through Ireland's 2002 World Cup soap opera, and acquired a sense of Roy Keane's temper. I now happen to be one of them.

I am not suggesting that someone who lives in a South American country or Japan would not understand this joke. Lest we forget, the news of Roy Keane being sent home was one of the dramatic highlights of the tournament. However, I want to argue that the reason why I, a Nigerian and not particularly a football fan could not resist laughing when I first set eyes on the T-shirt, are twofold. In the first place, the joke is based on the widely reported (more so in Ireland) event of Mick Mc Carthy, the manager of Ireland's national soccer team sending home his captain for vocal dissent. Secondly and probably more importantly, I have lived in Ireland long enough to know who Keane and McCarthy are, as well as the precarious relationship they had. I doubt if someone who does not live in or have any connection with Ireland would understand the full joke.

So, after eight years in Ireland, have I become a member of the 'imaginary circle' of people who would heartily laugh at a good Irish joke, in spite of the fact that I am non-native? The answer to that question is, Yes and No. I had lived in Nigeria for a quarter of a century before I began my sojourn abroad. In a sense, therefore, I am completely Nigerian. I now have cultivated a taste for Irish food, but I will prefer a Nigerian menu anytime. Also, I listen to all kinds of music but I prefer Nigerian artists. I mean, U2 might be one of the greatest bands in the world, but I am afraid their music does not resonate with me in the way Fela Kuti's does. For obvious reasons I speak in English all the time but I have no doubt in my mind that I will always be more fluent in my mother tongue, *Yoruba*. According to an African saying, 'The mangrove tree dwells in the river; that does not make it a crocodile'. My point, therefore, is that although I have gone through a process of cultural metamorphosis, deep down I still have a Nigerian point of view on things.

I remember, for instance, that when I saw a student production of J.M. Synge's, *The Playboy of the Western World,* not too long ago, it resonated with me on an entirely different emotional level as an outsider trying to come to terms with Irish culture. I had read somewhere before seeing the play that it caused a riot when it was first produced on the Abbey stage on the evening of the 26 January, 1907. Possibly, if I were Irish and a member of the audience that saw its first performance, I would have found Christy's reference to 'a drift of chosen females standing in their shifts' disrespectful enough to partake in that historical riot. Suffice it to say that Ireland has changed a great deal since then. These days, the controversial sexy lingerie shop, Ann Summers, shares the same O'Connell Street with the likes of Daniel O'Connell. So when I saw the play a couple of years ago, I failed (as I am sure most of the Irish audience also did) to see the point of the *hoola boola* over the first production of the play almost a century ago.

I did, however, see Christy Mahon as the epitome of a majority of immigrants constantly searching for who they are in a foreign land. For any immigrant to fit into a new environment, a lot of re-invention is necessary as Christy Mahon has demonstrated. As an African I personally know that fish loves water but not when it is boiling, so I do not blame anyone who seeks political or economic asylum in a Western country. I am nonetheless certain that the power to fabricate stories, tell them convincingly or even exaggerate them are all important skills for many to have, in order to strengthen their asylum applications. Why not? Is that not what Christy did? Because Christy Mahon re-invents himself, he is accorded the respect he truly deserves for the first time in his entire life and ultimately realizes his full potential. Is it not ironic though that when it is discovered that he is lying about killing his father, he becomes a nonentity all over again?

Despite the fact that I am a foreigner I have not failed to notice the cultural metamorphosis that Ireland has undergone in recent years. There are obviously many other cultural groups from Eastern Europe and Asia currently living in Ireland, but for obvious reasons I want to concentrate on Nigerians. It is reported there are about 30,000 Africans currently living in Ireland, compared to a couple of thousand about three years ago. Being the most populous and most politically unstable sub-Saharan African country, Nigerians are in the majority. As a Nigerian, I fully understand why anyone would want to abandon that country in search of a better life. For some strange reason, I could not help drawing a parallel between Christy's circumstances and the prevailing issue of asylum seekers and refugees in Ireland. That is probably why I see *The Playboy of the Western World* as more of a prophesy than a comedy.

Therefore, in order to ascertain how far I have come in decoding Irish comedy, I decided to go and see a play, regarded by everyone who has seen it, as very funny: *The Buddhist of Castleknock*. I went to see it one Saturday evening, and Andrews Lane Theatre was packed to its full capacity. (I was made to understand when I was booking my ticket, that I got the last available seat.) This is however hardly surprising since it was described by *The Sunday Tribune* as 'terrifically entertaining ... really funny'; by *The Examiner* as 'excellent ... hilarious, insightful and absolutely true ... laugh a minute success; and by *Rattlebag* as "highly recommended ...

fantastic ... hilarious'. The play, as it turned out was all of these things to almost everybody in the audience except me. I did not enjoy the play.

Buddhist tells the story of how the Sullivans, a seemingly cosy, middleclass Dublin family, deal with the intrusion of a stranger during a particular Christmas celebration. John, who lives in London, returns to Ireland accompanied by Rai, his black girlfriend, to celebrate the traditional Christmas with his parents, Sean and Edie and his siblings, Tara, Edward, and DJ. It seems that it is going to be like any other Christmas until John announces on Christmas eve that he is not going to attend Mass because he has converted to Buddhism, and, as a result, Christmas does not hold the same significance for him anymore. Instead of toeing the party line, Rai comes across as highly opinionated. In no time, she realizes that she has stepped beyond her boundaries and that her mere presence is a slap in the face to traditional Christmas festivity. Eventually she decides to go for a walk to give the family breathing space. She is later found by the police, after she has been beaten up in the park. The Sullivans, especially Tara, realize that if it had not been for their hostility towards their guest she would not have been assaulted. They apologize to Rai; bruised, battered and heavily bandaged, Rai returns to London with John. The play ends as Sean and Edie sit on the sofa, reflecting on how wonderful and 'not too quiet' that particular Christmas will be remembered. The round of applause that immediately followed the final blackout was deafening. And I remember that it took about three curtain calls for the applause to finally die down. That shows how much the audience enjoyed themselves in the theatre that evening. I unfortunately could not join in the enjoyment for the following reasons.

In the first place, being a foreigner, I could not help watching the play from Rai's point of view, and as a result feel her pain. Nor, at different moments in the play, could I help wondering if what was said about Rai was not the kind of things said by my Irish friends when my back is turned. This was actually a scary feeling because it was like a wake-up call for me. 'Watch your back always!' was the message I took from it. So, in a way, it was too close to my world to laugh at. How can I step far enough aside to find the notion that a black person can be attacked on the street at night something to laugh at? When Rai was brought back from the hospital, I found it strange that the audience still managed to find her situation funny. So it was not only that I did not find it funny, I found it a bit bothersome that other people found it funny. There were, nonetheless, some moments in the play that I have to admit I could not resist laughing at. For example, all the scenes with the young teenager, DJ, are extremely funny as he tries all the tricks in the book to break his family tradition. It is interesting also that as rebellious as the young character is portrayed, he is about the only one who does not see Rai as different or threatening. As Dermot Bolger writes in the play's programme, *The Buddhist of Castleknock*:

> ... depicts the thin veneer of unconscious racism within people whose outwardly comfortable lives allowed them the luxury of never having to confront such prejudices before, and the dangerous paralysis at the core of any family or society terrified of confronting change.

In a curious way, it is a similar theme, though that of sectarianism, which *A Night in November* explores in a powerful way. Employing the unforgettable experience of World Cup USA 1994 as a backdrop, and brilliantly acted by Marty Maguire, the play cleverly explores the divide and bitter rivalry that exist between the Protestant and Catholic communities in Northern Ireland. I have had the opportunity to travel on many occasions to Northern Ireland, so I am aware of how segregated the two communities are. As a matter of fact, anytime I am up North, I always feel that my guard is temporarily down because for that short period I am not seen as the 'other'. This, to a large extent, is why I think I enjoyed the play so much. The issue, this time, was between Catholics and Protestants – neither of which I am.

The play tells the story of how Kenneth Mc Callister, a member of the Protestant middle-class in Belfast, comes to terms with his Irishness. Like many other Protestants in Belfast, Kenneth strongly believes that he is superior to his Catholic counterparts because he leads an orderly life, he is a British citizen and also has a better job. But on the day a qualifying match is played between Northern

Ireland and the Republic of Ireland in Windsor Park, Kenneth begins to fathom what it means to be on the other side. It is obvious, on that day, that Windsor Park is not welcoming to Republic supporters and Belfast Catholics, as graffiti like, 'Taigs Keep Out', adorn the outside of the stadium. But during the match Kenneth notices that a Republican supporter is in their midst. Knowing full well what fate awaits the man if he is found out, Kenneth says, 'I was singing in his ears so that he would be safe from us'. The fact that the Republican supporter is not one of 'them' and as such is in danger simply because he happens to be a Catholic is unimaginable but real. And this is the reality that *A Night in November* explores skilfully. In a very odd way this reality has also become mine, because the main reason why I enjoyed the play was because I understood the references on which the play is based. There are many aspects of the play that I found really funny, but because of the scope of this essay I will limit myself to a few that still remain fresh in my memory.

When Kenneth decides to travel to the States to watch the boys in green it is hilarious. Firstly, he says, when he crossed the border, no one laughed mockingly at him. As a matter of fact, they offered him an Ireland jersey and taught him how to sing, 'We love you boys in Green', so that he would belong. To describe the sheer number of people that left Dublin for the States to see Ireland's World Cup matches, he says, 'they are more than the people who left during the famine'. But the funniest moment for me in the play has to be the description of Kenneth's experience when he gave Gerry, his Catholic workmate, a lift home because the latter's car was faulty. On their way, Kenneth says he mentioned to Gerry that it is funny they have never visited each other – but Gerry's response is that, 'it is not funny, it is weird'. It is also a bit weird that within the laughter there were moments in the play that were very poignant. The news that six people were killed watching the match in a pub in Ireland is one of such moments. When that line is delivered I am sure many did not know what to do, laugh or cry? The play ends with the powerful message, 'I am a Protestant but I am Irish'.

I am not Irish. But just like anyone who has lived in Ireland long enough, I am aware of the Troubles in the North, and therefore it was easy for me to follow the play from the beginning to the end. And for the first time I did not feel like an outsider watching an Irish play. Truly I might never be able to process or decode an Irish comedy as an Irish person would, but when I consider where I am now in comparison to where I was in my early days in Ireland, I have surely come a long way.

Sources

Bolger, Dermot, 'Programme Note' for *The Buddhist of Castleknock,* Fishamble, 2002.

Eco, Umberto, 'The Comic and the Rule' in *Faith in Fakes: Travels of Hyperreality*, trans. William Weaver (London: Minerva, 1995).

Freud, Sigmund, *Jokes and Their Relation to the Unconscious*, trans. James Strachey (Paperback, 1963).

Jones, Marie, *A Night in November* in *Stones in His Pockets* & *A Night in November* (London: Nick Hern, 2000).

Phillips, Adam, *The Joy of Sex and Laughter*, in *Index on Censorship*, vol.29, no. 6, November/December 2000.

8 | 'Good luck to ya': Fast-food Comedy at McDonagh's

Jan-Hendrik Wehmeyer

'No better place to witness the blood-dripping antics of Martin McDonagh than the Barbican Pit', I thought to myself ascending from its cavernous guts in London, after seeing the 2002 production of *The Lieutenant of Inishmore*; illicit chambers of torture always lay underground to muffle the cries of the dying. Just as the inviting glow of the Golden Arches suggests the instant delights of salty burgers, we can trust McDonagh to repel us into the perfidious pleasures of pain and shock. Both enjoyable, but of dubious nutritional value.

Such thoughts had already reared their heads after I attended McDonagh's *Lonesome West* in the sumptuous surroundings of Dublin's Gaiety Theatre. Having laughed my socks off together with rest of the house – when obviously we shouldn't have, as Coleman pointedly remarks – I was deeply thankful for my 9-to-5 setup in the cosy environs of Dublin where no such hideous characters as McDonagh's could interfere with my sanity or even safety.

Something sinister appears to be at work in McDonagh's plays, something beyond the implosions of all traditional notions of Oirish-ness on which he plays so successfully. Why *do* we laugh when we obviously shouldn't? Who do we laugh at? Have I sold out to the comforts of unchecked cynicism? Do McDonagh's plays change perceptions of the world depicted? Or indeed the one I am living in? What interests do they serve?

Martin McDonagh's plays – The Leenane Trilogy, The Cripple of Inishmaan and The Lieutenant of Inishmore, as of this writing – depict repellent and ethically despicable small-town antics where no redemption appears possible. The characters populating Leenane and the remote islands in a fictional West of Ireland put to shame even the most outlandish Jerry Springer cast. Not a moral voice breaks through this jungle except, perhaps, Father Walsh's (or was it Welsh?) drunken whisper of God's jurisdiction before disappearing from the audience's world.

It may be territory already visited by Synge, et al., but, whereas Christy Mahon walks off the stage into a brighter future, Father Whatever stumbles straight into the cold grave of the Leenane waters, to be remembered only by the vol-au-vents at his funeral. Just like Synge and Yeats and others credited with the Irish Literary Revival, McDonagh is somewhat a stranger to the place where he lays his scenes.

McDonagh's parents belonged to the 'Irish exiled' in England. They were from Sligo and Galway and he was born and raised in London, in the Elephant and Castle area, with his wider family and other Irish families living all around him. The McDonaghs' summer holidays were spent in Ireland, in the region in which Leenane is situated, County Sligo and Connemara. When his parents moved back to Ireland, he stayed behind. He joined the Catholic parish choir and was undoubtedly immersed in countless stories of home, Irish nationalism and folk tales. At the same time, McDonagh could hardly have escaped the global urban culture of London, the slang of different ethnic groups, U.S. movies and television shows that dominate dramatic output.

McDonagh is as much 'outside' his subject matter as the Anglo-Irish were at the beginning of the last century. Thomas Kilroy observes in his article, 'The Anglo-Irish Theatrical Imagination', that these descendants of English settlers in Ireland were characterized by a culture in suspension between 'other, irreconcilable cultures, the parent English on the one side and the native Irish on the other'. Kilroy calls this a 'see-saw' condition of being 'in-between' two cultures, and the artistic attempt to struggle towards a condition of wholeness. The binary opposition necessitates 'ingenious strategies of survival and adaptation, of masking, mimicry and rhetorical finesse': Christy Mahon's intellectual eloquence is cloaked in the rugged fabric of the country peasant.

The main strategy of such mimicry is to create a cool and removed distance between the playwright and his subject matter. Such creative distancing means that the playwrights, for the most part, chose not their own social and cultural fabric to be the material of their plays. Synge and Yeats, for example, grew up in a distinct Protestant environment, yet their material – peasants, tinkers, Celtic mythology – could not be more removed from a 'genteel background'. Such 'creative distancing' favours the emblematic, the artificial construct of present – a simulacrum in postmodern vocabulary; the simulation of a reality that never actually existed in the first place.

Central to this Anglo-Irish imagination is the 'outside' vision, which allows alertness to nuances of cultural activities because they are viewed not exclusively from within them, but from the outside and mediated through the Other element of the hybrid consciousness.

McDonagh may be perceived to fit this bill. As an Irish native living in London, his material is outside his immediate experience. He 'knows' about it just like Synge: through 'cracks of the floorboard', overhearing conversations, picking up impressions and then processing and distancing these through the imagination. Yet McDonagh's imagination is a hybrid cultural consciousness, which is not defined by a binary opposition – Irish/English – but by a multitude of 'oppositions'. This hybrid consciousness appears to mediate his sense of Irishness, disrupting and further distancing it: The traditional Irish family meets Hollywood's bloody battlegrounds. Violent showdowns, brutal and arguably gratuitous killing of family members à la Tarantino, and blood baths caused by a half-wit INLA kid co-exist with the relentless foregrounding of references to Tayto's, Complan and Eamonn Andrews. All this is glued together by mock Irishisms in a language which mimics an Irish texture: 'Is it a biteen more craic yer wantin', so?' Hilarious stuff this. Not only to be enjoyed by the true-born inhabitants of the country, but also by non-natives like myself who now call Ireland home; not to mention audiences from Poland to Pittsburgh. Such global success is ensured by the universality that characterizes McDonagh's comic devices.

The most basic of these is undoubtedly the device of mis-appropriation, most beautifully realised in the famine joke in the *Skull of Connemara*. In this passage, Mick teases Mairtin over his question of where the 'thing', i.e. penis, goes, when being buried:

> **Mick:** [...] Isn't it illegal in the Catholic faith to bury a body the willy still attached? Isn't it a sin in the eyes of the Lord?
> **Mairtin:** (*incredulous*) No ...
> **Mick:** Don't they snip them off in the coffin and sell them to tinkers as dog food?
> **Mairtin:** (*horrified*) They do not!
> **Mick:** And during the famine, didn't the tinkers stop feeding them to their dogs at all and start sampling the merchandise themselves?
> **Mairtin:** They did not, now, Mick ...
> **Mick:** You would see them riding along with them, munching ahead.
> Mairtin: No ...
> **Mick:** That's the trouble with young people today, is they don't know the first thing about Irish history.

The distance between the banter about the male sexual organ and the tragedy of the Irish famine, the most sacred collective Irish memory, is too great to be bridged rationally. Laughter is the only release mechanism.

McDonagh excels in the juxtaposition of the mundane and shocking. Stunning in its visual grotesqueness is a scene in the *Lieutenant* where Padraic is just about to kill his friend Davey and his dad when 'old friends' surprisingly pop in for a visit.

> **Padraic:** Christy! What the feck are you fellas doing out this way? Come in ahead for yourselves. I'm just in the middle of shooting me dad. He *turns his back on them, goes back to the two kneeling men and points his guns at their heads, at the same time as the three men at the door dash in, take guns out from behind their backs and point them right up against Padraic's head – one on the left side, one on the right and one from behind, in something of a triangle.*
>
> **Padraic:** (*Pause*) What's all this about, now?
> **Christy:** Does the word 'splinter group' mean anything to ya?

Padraic: 'Splinter group'? 'Splinter group''s two words. (McDonagh, 2001, 45)

A beautiful triangle emerges on stage, framing an unholy cross of guns with mad Padraic at its centre. It is the sheer absurdity of the situation – murdering friend and father – infused by the all too familiar image of insane gunmen acting in the name of obscure republican splinter groups which forces our laughter. 'The ghosts are rattling at the cage' – we can almost hear Shane McGowan whistling from the wings – 'and the devil's in the chair'. Not surprisingly by the end of the night, most of the personnel on stage will have found a grotesquely bloody end.

McDonagh ruthlessly blends the grotesque with the familiar, visually, as well as in language, effortlessly fusing talk of a trip to Leisureland and the battering of a wife's skull. Mick is holding the skull of his wife as he converses with Maryjohnny and Mairtin Hanlon:

> **Mairtin:** I suppose that'd be your missus, would it, Mick?
> **Mick:** It would.
> **Mairtin:** Uh-huh. Has she changed much since last you saw her?
> **Mick:** (*Pause*) She has, Mairtin.
> **Mairtin:** Oh aye, it's been seven years, I suppose.
> **Mary:** Do you like bumpy slides, Mairtin?
> **Mairtin:** Bumpy slides? Where the hell did bumpy bloody slides come from?
> **Mary:** I won two goes on the bumpy slides at Leisureland if you'd want to go.
> **Mairtin:** You won't catch me going on the bumpy slides with you, missus. I'd look a pure fool.
> **Mary:** No, you could bring somebody else, I'm saying. (*She gives Mairtin the tickets.*)
> **Mairtin:** Oh. Aye. Thank you, Gran. Maybe Mona'd want to go. Heh, this has been a great oul day, this has. Drinking and driving and bumpy slides, and that oul battering them skulls to skitter was the best part of the whole day. (McDonagh, 1999, 124)

As in most comedy, characterization is shallow. The characters are crudely carved and don't seem to be framed in an emotional landscape which is recognizable to the audience. Emotional interaction is thus reduced to the lowest common denominator on the emotional palette – pain as caused by psychological and physical violence: 'It shows that you care', proclaims Valene in the *Lonesome West.*

Indeed, a lot of such caring goes on in McDonagh's plays. Violence is ubiquitous and excessive, in language, as well as physically. The second Act of the *Lieutenant* must easily rate as the bloodiest ever staged since Shakespeare let Titus loose on Rome; corpses being sawed into bits, skulls kicked around and eyes shot out. Pain through excessive violence in McDonagh's plays becomes an almost normal condition. The plot does not easily justify such excessiveness. It becomes sensational, rendering the once ritualistic 'killing off' of the Powers that Be in drama emptied and devoid of any meaning. The excess of violence and pain as a normal state loses its transformative and cathartic power, becomes aesthetic and sensational and is as such gratuitous.

In such an emotional desert, meaningful relationships are absent. Girleen's tame attempt to console Father Welsh is belied by his subsequent suicide, Maureen's relation to Pato is largely motivated by offering her the possibility of escaping her horrific mother, and Donny's shy display of sympathy over Padraic's dead cat can easily be read as sarcasm – there is not much room to imagine redemption in human bonds. Each to their own in McDonagh's world, resulting in the angular and misconstrued vision of each character, expressed on stage by their admittedly hilarious oddity. What does this offer us, the audience? Does our laughter offer a changed perception; does it indicate a transformational quality of play on McDonagh's stage?

A powerful transformational quality of play is subversion through irony and parody as a temporary liberation of commonly known and prevailing truths. Parodying the Powers that Be thus has a repression-release function, helping us to cope with the perceived terrifying norm. A great moment of such carnivalesque play is the temporary wealth granted to Juno and Captain Boyle in Sean O'Casey's *Juno and the Paycock*, which is then cruelly taken away, exposing the deficiencies of the characters and society. All this happens against the backdrop of a recognizable, prevailing 'reality' created by the stage action and setting. Juno and the Captain's sudden wealth framed within their actual 'reality' of poverty, exemplifies such distinctions.

Mikhail Bakhtin points out the relation of carnivalesque fest-ivities to moments of crisis and breaking points in the cycle of nature and society and men. Moments of death and revival, of change and renewal always lead to a festive perception of the world. Play in this sense is linked with a possibility of 'becoming, change and renewal.' The possibility of distinguishing between these two worlds places the audience in a position to make choices, to judge what is happening, to validate or reject decisions. In other words, audiences are allowed intervention, which may have transformative powers on the spectator.

This is not the case in McDonagh. A distinction between the real and play is no longer clearly visible. Play, with all its attributes of excess and liberating mimicry is not distinctly framed within a tangible reality to which an audience can relate. In a sense, carnival, characterized in McDonagh by parody and excessive spectacle becomes a permanent condition. The excess becomes the norm. Only by accepting the presented characters as different from ourselves, as inferior, as our Other are we able to laugh at their hideousness. As a result, we are happier in our current position and have shed even the last bit of our questioning powers. Is there a judgement to be made on Padraic's torturing and killings? Or on Maureen's blasting apart her mother's skull? Or on Johnny-pateenmike's poisonings?

What is drawing us to these plays? Given their commercial suc-cess, audiences must feel a distinct affinity with McDonagh's imagination. As suggested, it is always easy to laugh at your in-feriors, and the sometimes pointed and witty dialogue does its part to give the plays their appeal. But does this make McDonagh 'shallow'?

Despite the oddity and angularity of McDonagh's world, we feel we know very well what's 'going on'. At times, through McDonagh's eyes, we can glimpse the cruelty to which isolation and disenfranchisement can push people, in news reports of kill-ings and beatings within what we may think are closely knit com-munities. Authors at their best write about what they know. McDonagh knows about the rough rural isolated world of the West of Ireland and the characters that populate it by earwigging and eavesdropping during visits to Connemara and in the company of Irish exiles.

But 'knowing' does not mean 'comprehending'. In McDonagh, the complexities of the small world of our experience appear to be overwhelming and more impossible to transcend than at the time of Synge and Yeats. A hundred years on, the instant gratification of laughter and sensory overload – high-calorie junk – seems to have won the day.

McDonagh's cold distance reveals a lack of comprehension of what drives his folks, a lack shared, possibly, by myself and a sizable chunk of his audience. Only compassion-free observation and description, cruel fingerpointing at exaggerated deficiencies seems possible. Relentlessly he deprives us of touches of humanity, not to mention empowering visions. With McDonagh we are only ever one foot above the grave. If we accept such passive attitudes, his comedy cements the agonizing prevailing lunacy it seems to mock and undermine. Facing such a cage of mere existence, we are tempted to agree with Girleen's contemplation of live and death:

> But at least when you're still here there's the possibility of happiness, and it's like them dead ones know that, and they're happy for you to have it, – not exactly an action plan for happiness – 'they say "Good luck to ya" '.

Is she not asking us to accept the unacceptable? The sardonic smile on Girleen's face seems to mirror McDonagh's as she is releasing the audience into the cold night; in search of more burgers.

Sources:

Eagleton, Terry, *The Illusions of Postmodernism* (Oxford: Blackwell, 1996).
McDonagh, Martin, *Plays: 1* (London: Methuen, 1999).
---------- *The Cripple of Inishmaan* (London: Methuen, 1997).
---------- *The Lieutenant of Inishmore* (London: Methuen, 2001).
Kilroy, Thomas, 'The Anglo-Irish Theatrical Imagination' in *Bullán. An Irish Studies Journal*, Vol.III, No.2 (Winter 1997/Spring 1998), pp.5-12.

9 | I A Clown

Raymond Keane

I love clown. I hate clown.

I was born at six o'clock in the morning. My mother tells me I woke the whole house up including herself. I totally believed this for years. In a way, I still kind of do … or want to.

My first experience of clown, like most people, was at the circus. I cried. The clown car exploded and fell apart. I cried. One clown hit another. I cried. Bozo the clown dumped a bucket of confetti over me. I cried. Mind you, I cried at the trapeze act, the lion tamer, the knife thrower, the loud music and almost everything else, bar the ice cream and the candy floss, but I'll never forget my fear of those clowns. I had a similar experience at my first movie. It was a Laurel and Hardy. Laurel was boarding a boat on a quayside. With one foot on the quayside and the other on the boat while it drifted outwards, his fear of the inevitable became mine. His final feat I cannot recount for I was up and out of the cinema running and crying all the way home, in futile and inconsolable pursuit by my minder sister.

Some of my own clown performance experiences have had the same effect on younger audiences, particularly in my early days of street theatre. Many parents would encourage and even physically urge their children, 'Say Hello to the *funny* clown', while I would discreetly, yet desperately, try to communicate, 'No, no, *scary* clown, *scary* clown'. Securing a safer distance between us, I never could decide which I felt most sorry for, the child, the parent, or myself. Maybe it's because the child was once my experience (and it still lives somewhere in here), I am now the instigator of the experience, and the parent is the conundrum. Coupled with my childhood fear and dread of slapstick clown I have vivid memories of Sunday afternoons filled with tears of laughter streaming down my face while watching Buster Keaton, Charlie Chaplin and the Marx Brothers on the telly. The skill and madness of Harpo, the deadpan and death-defying brilliance of Keaton and the virtuosity, pathos and physical acting of Chaplin remain a mystery to me to this day.

At the age of five an accidental altercation with the door of a car left me with four and a half fingers on my right hand. It was brilliant. No memory of any pain. Fell in love with my nurse in the hospital. A freak show, the centre of attention. The gags came fast and furious, picking my nose still my all-time favourite. Never missed it until the early days of mime school, finger exercises, the wall, stuffing that white glove became an obsession.

My fifth-class teacher at the Christian Brothers school in Dungarvan may have been a huge (albeit inadvertent) influence on my chosen path towards clownhood. His peculiarly perverted form of punishment – and as far as I can remember, reserved only for yours truly – was to paint my nose with a red biro. A rather mild form of punishment, you might think, for an Irish Catholic boys' school in the mid-Sixties; but when coupled with the strict order of non-removal until presented and viewed by my parents, it took on a whole new consequence, or at least, was supposed to. However, it was greeted with more anger towards the perpetrator than me by my parents, elevating my alleged wrongdoing to a human-rights issue. Their solidarity made me feel extremely proud of them. I can also recall a deep sense of pride in my painted red nose, its anti-establishment status perhaps, but also the laughter, pathos and puzzlement it seemed to elicit from its audience. If that was my introduction to red-nose clown, then thank you very much Bro'.

My love of the red-nose clown thing is sometimes beyond my comprehension. It is not the only form of theatre I practice but it informs almost everything I do. It is, of course a mask, *the smallest mask in the world,* Lecoq would call it. But then again, isn't all or at least most theatre a form of mask? In simple effect, the red nose heightens or makes bigger. This small red sphere at first seems to dominate the face but when embodied reveals the clown within the wearer. It does not automatically make the wearer funny, and in some will have the opposite effect. It can, however, prove a very valuable friend indeed. This 'inner clown' has a lot to offer for comedy but equally as much for tragedy. If the wearer is inherently funny, then the mask may intensify their funniness; an equal intensification may occur if the wearer is inherently tragic. The tragic clown, though, can also offer huge potential for comedy. Through this exquisite red-sphere mask we can laugh and cry, at and with our humanity in all its love, joy, truth, innocence, gullibility, vulnerability, fear, failure, curiosity, humility and magic. In the heightened reality of the clown world we are allowed to view our more extreme selves at a safe distance. The mask, like all masks, seems to provide an extra margin of removal, while, at the same time, allowing us to experience those extremes with greater potency. In essence, I propose, it offers us a glimpse at the clown within ourselves.

In my years of facilitating and participating in clown workshops I continue to be intrigued by the enormous challenges the clown presents for participants of all backgrounds and training approaches: the struggle, the frustration, the nakedness and, if and when the penny drops, the ultimate joy the mask elicits. Actors, dancers and performers of all persuasions find something of value they can integrate into their creative processes. There are some, of course, for whom the clown thing makes absolutely no sense – and this can be of enormous value to their creative processes. The recognition and acceptance that a particular discipline has nothing to offer can be a hugely liberating experience for any practitioner. There is no point in barking up the wrong tree when you could be sucking chestnuts only fifty feet away.

Although I had practised and performed as a clown for a number of years, it was not until the formation of my present company, Barabbas, that the penny really and finally dropped for me. That said, it continues to drop on a sometimes shockingly regular basis. Barabbas was founded in 1993 by me, Veronica Coburn and Mikel Murfi. We set about making a theatre that was a combination of the three of our backgrounds and experiences. At the core of all three of our backgrounds was the delight in and love of theatre of clown. There is a story I like to relate, which may or may not be theatrical myth, but it tickles me no end. It goes like this: When John B. Keane first presented his play, *Sharon's Grave*, to our National Theatre, it is reported that the artistic director rejected it on the grounds that you couldn't have a play with three idiots in it, one being the maxim in classical tradition. Well, in Barabbas we delight in the premise that we formed a whole company on the basis of three idiots. Idiots, fools and eejits would find a welcome in the house of Barabbas, a cup of tea if they were willing to hang out a while, and a chip butty if they had anything at all to say for themselves.

The search for the clown within according to Saint Barabbas.

… and nine months later Raymond Clown was re-born. Veronica, Mikel and Raymond jumped into bed together, in a purely professional way, I hasten to add (although no money changed hands). It was a warm, comfortable bed with hard bits, lumpy bits and some soft bits. I liked being in the middle a lot where I could spoon and be spooned at the same time – nice! – safe! – secure! – or so I thought. And it was all these things, but it was also immensely challenging, difficult and inspiring. In this womblike, 'embro-clownic' existence I experienced a form of re-birthing, and re-discovered the soul of Raymond Clown.

Are clowns funny?

Well, funniness is certainly a proposition the clown makes. Isn't it? Or is it? They can also be bad, sad, even evil. It seems, however, that we are conditioned, for whatever reason, to expect funniness from clowns. Why then do some people find clowns the un-funniest thing ever? I know people who would prefer to swallow a bicycle raw rather than watch a clown performance. In some cases I can understand why, which may stem from my own early childhood aversion. These days I am somewhat better equipped to articulate and understand that reaction. In my humble opinion it is simply down to the 'good' and the 'crap'. Good Clowns Inc v Crap Clowns Anonymous. Have you ever been approached, nay, ac-costed, and I'm on a roll here, by a big-wigged, brightly clad, bigshoed, badly made-up clown on the street (or anywhere for that matter) and had an uncontrollable urge to slapstick him or her into early retirement? Well I have. On the other hand, have you ever been touched by an angel, torn by your heart, transfixed in beauty, transported in joy, terrified with fear, taught by laughter, tested by honesty, tenderized by gullibility, troubled in truth, tickled with curiosity, treated by magic, and sometimes all at the same time? I have, and where I have most often is in the presence of a master clown. So, are clowns funny? Yes, but only when they are. Why is one clown funnier than another? Because that's the way the cookie crumbles.

So, is Raymond Clown a funny clown?

Maybe, has been sometimes, and hopefully will be again, but I wouldn't say he is a *very* funny clown. As much as Raymond Clown likes to make people laugh, he does not always succeed – but sometimes being unsuccessful is also funny. Back again in early Barabbas days, Veronica used to have a theory which I'm sure she still believes. She used to say that Mikel Clown 'was a funny', Raymond Clown 'tried to be funny' and Veronica Clown 'was just not funny'. In my opinion her theory is half right and half wrong. However, the most interesting half is the right half. It is a valuable quest, for most performers, in finding out how funny they actually are, and, of course, of considerably more significance for comedians and clowns. The red-nose mask is a remarkable tool for this process. The mask: If the character mask reveals the character, the red-nose mask reveals the wearer, and eventually the clown within the wearer. There is a much-used exercise by clown teachers and clown facilitators around the world, in which students are asked to leave the room and, on return, simply to *be funny*. It is a very scary task for most performers. One of its purposes is to expose the inevitable failure which, when accepted, becomes a great friend to performer and clown. Failure can be a good starting point – at least you know things can't get much worse. Failure for a clown is commonplace. Failure for Raymond Clown, or maybe just Raymond, is a miraculous gift. Finding comfort in that failure takes a huge weight off the shoulders of both of us and provides us with a springboard for endless possibility.

Come Down From The Mountain John Clown, John Clown was Barabbas's debut show and the first outing of Veronica Clown, Mikel Clown and Raymond Clown. Veronica Clown, supported by a 'start your own business scheme', made and sold sandwiches on the street. Well, 'sold', is a bit of an exaggeration. In fact, she never sold even one. I suspect the public weren't quite ready for her unusually artistic culinary interpretations. Indeed her sandwiches were a work of art (in her eyes anyway). One of Veronica Clown's moments of true bliss was her compassion and empathy for a tomato as she prepared one of her sandwiches. Before she sliced it, she was compelled to anaesthetize it by injection. The moments she waited for the anaesthetic to take effect on this small red sphere were the sweetest, before testing its numbness with a metal hammer. Veronica, herself, once had a job in a well-known, upmarket Dublin hotel. One of her main duties was shaping butter into small spirals. Another was spraying the jelly desserts from the fridge to make them look appetizing before serving. I can only see the picture with her wearing her red nose.

Mikel Clown was a T.V. reporter in the show. His daily assignments consisted of him interviewing his glove puppet by the name of 'Bart Chicken' outside government buildings. It was every reporter's nightmare, in which one mistake inspired another. The laughter, vulnerability and ultimate pathos we the audience experienced are impossible to convey in words. Mikel *had* worked in television, and his abiding memory was of his fear and failure as an interviewer.

Raymond Clown belonged to the long-term unemployed, or maybe the unemployable. He filled his days with mostly happy thoughts under the constant presence of 'cloud reality'. His highlight of the week was Dole Day, when he collected his social welfare payment of five pounds, and where his battle with bureaucracy became his nemesis. His return journey would take him through the park, where he always encountered a pond full of hungry and persistent ducks. Raymond Clown's compassion always got the better of him, as he gave his five pounds to the ducks with the instruction that they buy a sliced pan between them. Raymond Clown was not the brightest spark, and that's enough said about that.

John Clown was married to Veronica Clown but never appeared in the show. He worked as a chef on an oil rig. Each morning a letter from him would arrive with news of his latest menu options. His excitement of serving such exotic culinary delights as melon slices was palpable. One afternoon an ominous telegram arrives from the oil rig. It carried but four words – 'JOHN CLOWN IS DEAD'. Veronica, Mikel and Raymond Clown set about their own particular brand of ritual to mourn his passing. It was both gut-wrenchingly sad and hilarious at the same time, proving that even death can be a very funny thing. One of my abiding memories from childhood is attending funerals where comedy was not high on the list of appropriate experiences. For some inane and usually inexplicable reason I would find myself in a fit of giggles. The more I tried to suppress them the stronger they became until I lost all control. Now, for me, that is pure comedy.

Sick Dying Dead Buried Out was the title of our second clown show. (What's with this death thing?) However, in this case, the death part was not that funny at all. The opening scene had a clown (me) hanging upside down dead. Devised by the three of us, directed by Veronica, and performed by Mikel and me, it explored the relationship between two friends, Ulti and Pauri, who grew up together and fulfilled their destinies of becoming clowns. Red spheres of all descriptions took on great significance from a very young age. We saw the characters in their 'real-life' personas, and followed their careers from humble and crude beginnings to the heights of their creativity and eventual demise. Their best and funniest sketch was in a bath. A bath full of water and bubbles was wheeled onstage. I appeared and prepared to take a bath by first undressing. Realizing the audience had full view – clowns realize these things far more often than characters in 'real' plays – I decided to leave my underpants on until I was safely in the bath. I then removed them, squeezed them out, hung them on the side of the bath, and began to bathe. I lost a bar of soap in the water, but immediately found it (not always an easy feat at the best of times). This action was repeated a number of times throughout. The phone rang persistently, and I was eventually compelled to answer it. I had to put my underpants back on in the bath before I got out. I did and, of course, just missed the call as I picked up the receiver, which proved mildly annoying. I returned to my bath and repeated the underpants routine. No sooner had I settled back in, but the doorbell rang, also persistently. The process was repeated, and this time I bought a vacuum cleaner from an unseen salesman. By now the audience got the impression that the phone caller and salesman was Mikel playing tricks on me. Anyway, I returned in the same fashion to continue to bathe. The audience should now have been ahead of themselves, wondering what would be the next ploy to get me out of the bath. Good gags usually come in threes, but this time took a more bizarre turn. A shark fin appeared above the water, and swam around the bath, accompanied by the *Jaws* theme – then a periscope from a submarine, and finally a hand clutching a bar of soap (in fact, one I had lost in fright from the shark fin). By now I had enough and decided to dive under to investigate. (It is important to know that thirteen minutes had passed since the sketch had begun.) Anyway, I put on some goggles and dove under. I resurfaced, now accompanied by Mikel. We stared each other in the face while the audience screamed. We then, for some unexplainable reason, performed a synchronized swimming routine, as the audience tried to figure out what they had just seen. We had pulled off a *coup de théâtre*, and the audience appreciated it every time.

It is this kind of trickery and invention that sets my heart alight in theatre and is so perfectly compatible with the world of play: surprise and magic in the theatre of clown. Most theatre forms deal in the unexpected; for the clown, nothing is what is expected, nothing is what it seems, and at the same time everything is just exactly as it says it is. If it says it's going to rain cats and dogs, the clown believes it will rain cats and dogs. The great clown masters say that clown is not a technique, but rather a state. Just like real life I suppose, and isn't life a funny thing after all?

As I mentioned earlier, the theatre of clown is not the only form of theatre I practice but does form the basis for everything else I do. It has taught me to wait and recognize those inspirational comic moments that can only be found through play. Then, of course, the work really begins, in capturing it in rehearsal and finding a way to let it sparkle each night on stage.

10 | Comic Patterns in *Kevin's Bed* and *Twenty Grand*

Eric Weitz

No playwright begins from scratch, least of all the comic playwright.

Writing in thrall to the conventions of a particular culture in time, the playwright draws from a toolbox of forms and strategies acquired (consciously and otherwise) since childhood. Stock structures, characters and patterns can be detected in the X-ray of every stage world. Combined with the actualities of production, they provide cues to the spectator as to how to process the events being depicted (is this supposed to be funny?), and to construct expectations (will the heroine attain her goal?).

Interestingly, comedy's basic instructional kit – including character types and punchline patterns – has not changed all that much since the ancient Greeks and Romans. Comic performance palettes have reached us in various shapes from the *commedia dell'arte*. Genres have interpenetrated and regenerated to engage comedy in new configurations, but humour strategies remain recognizable from era to era and place to place in Western practice. We may find them more embedded in the habits of performance and spectating than we realize.

Kevin's Bed, by Bernard Farrell and *Twenty Grand*, by Declan Hughes, played in the Abbey and Peacock theatres respectively in 1998, and show something of how Western comedy is still and always built by local artisans upon the broadest historical templates. The two playwrights render their stage worlds in cultural languages which would read as North and Southside subcultures in turn-of-the-21st-century Dublin. Although the joking material is locally specific, the joking forms are fairly familiar, as are the comic performance patterns they support.

This essay will visit a series of recognizable strategies in one or both of the plays under discussion: the so-called 'Coventry' joke; the defective exchange; the defamiliarization of everyday idiom; a juxtaposition of genre and character status; the comic pairing; and the effective withdrawal of joking conditions.

Playwright Bernard Farrell has shown consistent proficiency in the technique of comic writing. His worlds are comfortably familiar as potential slices of contemporary Irish life, and would usually be perceived as not particularly tendentious in comedy and theme. Their humour relies on socio-cultural references, generally uncontroversial biases and classic situational ironies. Usually, some emotional issue of contemporary socio-cultural experience lies at the crux of the play.

His play, *Kevin's Bed*, takes place entirely in the kitchen of a house in Dublin, during anniversary parties for Kevin's parents 'today' and twenty-five years ago. Kevin is twenty-two years old in the first act and suddenly returned from the Irish College of Rome, having reneged on an earlier decision to enter the priesthood. The fact emerges that Kevin's Italian-speaking guest, Maria, is not a nun come to counsel him about returning to the priesthood, but a young woman with whom he is in love and who now carries his child. Much first-act comic action sees Kevin, then his brother, and eventually his father, trying to keep Maria's real identity from his starchy mother. Kevin must also deal with the confused attentions of Betty, his brother's fiancée who might once have had a claim on his affection. All pretence unravels in a first-act finale, to Kevin's mother's expected displeasure. In the second act, twenty-five years later, Kevin and Maria are married, with a grown daughter, but their lives clearly have not stayed the path of true love in the wake of their love-child's birth. Kevin's father convinces the boys that their mother has but a short time to live; eventually, however, he reveals that it was a hoax, his way of seeing that *this* anniversary party goes off without any undesirable intrigue to upset Mom. Ultimately Kevin is left in rather downbeat condition, having made a final tentative effort to rekindle a spark with Betty. The original production was directed by Ben Barnes, getting full comic value from a cast which included Eamon Morrissey as Kevin's father, Dan, and David Parnell as Kevin.

Staking out somewhat different territory, Declan Hughes' *Twenty Grand* shows how comic devices pitch darker fabrics. It unfolds along the lines of a gangsterish genre of fiction and cinema, violent and glib, identified originally with writers like Raymond Chandler and given a 1990s cynicism by filmmaker Quentin Tarantino. Here it was retooled for Northside Dublin, the production directed by Conal Morrison with the genre's characteristic staccato rhythms and hair-trigger threat of brutality. The plot of the play sees an underground kingpin named Hackett, going about the sordid business of trying to discover who in his circle has pocketed the missing 'twenty grand' of the title. Dalton, an apparent neophyte gang member and boyfriend of Hackett's daughter, arrives in the boss' penthouse lair to watch a suspected traitor tortured and beaten over the missing money. Recriminations fly in all directions, with Hackett's son and another gang member present. Eventually, deadly violence takes over, and, with only Hackett left (barely) alive onstage, Dalton reveals that his callow persona had been a chameleonlike ploy to get him inside Hackett's den and confidence. Dalton's sudden show of steel, savvy, and stomach for violence turn the stage world upside down, as chillingly he takes up his position at the top of the pile. The cast included Liam Carney as Hackett, Karl Shiels as his son, Dean, and Anthony Brophy as Dalton.

It may be true that all jokes are 'private', in that they rely on shared, unspoken references – but they are also in some way universal in (Western) construction. A simple method by which a playwright exploits 'private' reference from the stage is through what Walter Nash calls the 'Coventry' joke, which invokes some sort of debasement of a locally recognized place or its people. Hughes spins such a variation in *Twenty Grand*, early in the play, in a scene between Hackett and Dalton:

> **Hackett:** ... Ah, it's all fucked up out there anyway.
> **Dalton:** In Bray? Yeah.
> **Hackett:** Why is that, d'you think?
> **Dalton:** That they're all fucked up out in Bray?
> **Hackett:** Yeah.
> **Dalton:** I don't know.
> **Hackett:** Suppose it's on account of spending all day out in fucking Bray.

A spectator from outside the greater Dublin area may recognize the joke type better than the butt, and will still be able to get its point. As Nash suggests:

> It shows that we are not required to have the *specific* experience to which the witticism refers, but only to grasp a category, to recognise the *kind* of image that is raised. (Nash, 13)

This is a joke that anyone can 'get'. It is not necessary to share Hackett's feeling towards Bray in order to respond to this gag. The feeling of this joking pattern is most likely ingrained in the spectator, who may even laugh at the joke without completely 'getting' it (thereby laughing without even knowing why Bray should be an object of derision). For the knowing spectator, however, the culturally 'private' recognition might provide a special spark of inclusive pleasure.

Farrell also exploits the specialized signifier in *Kevin's Bed*. In Act I, the widowed Pauline, a friend of Dan and Doris (Kevin's parents), is now keeping company with Cyril, of whom she says wistfully, 'oh, that's just companionship, Doris – no one could ever take the place of Tim'. The sentiment, apparently earnest as played by Marion O'Dwyer, is reinforced many times during the act. In the second act, twenty-five years on and now with Cyril behind her as well, Pauline describes her latest relationship, attempting to make it sound more platonic than romantic. Her latest beau is Reggie, a Northerner from Lurgan, who is divorced:

> **Doris:** Divorced?
> **Pauline:** ... and I didn't like to hear that either – but it's only for companionship, because nobody could ever take the place of poor Cyril.
> **Doris:** ... of course not ...

> **Pauline:** ... and I know Lurgan is a bit of a distance – but the way we work it is: this fortnight Reggie comes down to me and the next fortnight I go up to him.
> **Dan:** Home and away, Pauline, just like Manchester United.

Dan slices through Pauline's attempt at demure downplaying of the relationship with a 'real-life' reference to the scheduling patterns of a popular English football club – in which the winner of a match-up is decided over the course of two games, one played in each team's home stadium ('home and away'). Again, for the initiated, Dan's metaphor throws up an incongruous pairing of Pauline and a bunch of professional male athletes, while inferring a comparison of her 'innocent' friendship to the rugged physical contact of a football pitch.

Another familiar comic strategy precipitated verbally lies in 'defective exchange' contrived by the playwright. This works by way of a humorous misdirection brought on by some violation of H.P. Grice's maxims for 'ordinary' conversation (what amounts to a bunch of guidelines whereby speakers tacitly agree to use language fairly). As summarized by Nash, they include:

> the obligation to give adequate and accurate information, not to be prolix, not to get into conversational deadlocks, not to be snagged on *non-sequiturs*, to pay attention to what is said, to try to make relevant assertions and responses. (Nash, 116)

Early in the first act of *Kevin's Bed*, Dan gives vent to impatience with Kevin. John (Kevin's brother) and Doris (their mother), in Kevin's defence, are trying to tell Dan about the surprise arrival of a visitor from Rome, whom they both believe to be a nun:

> **Doris:** He's done nothing ...
> **John:** It's not bad news, da.
> **Dan:** Everything about that fellow is bad news ...
> **Doris:** ... Dan ...
> **Dan:** 'I want to be a Christian Brother, I don't want to be a Christian Brother; I want to be a priest, I don't want to be a priest.'
> **John:** No da, this news is different.
> **Doris:** This is news about a nun.
> **Dan:** Jaysas, don't tell me he now wants to be a nun!

This sort of defective exchange reveals the inadvertent mischief wreaked upon our sophisticated communicative procedures when they come under pressure. It remains a signal feature of farcical worlds, which are generally rigged for misunderstanding through crossed plots and the desperation of evasion.

One can trace the progress of the misdirection and its comic consequences; each conversant incurs a minor infraction of the Gricean rules, until Dan wilfully misapprehends the subject of the second to last sentence. The confusion is made more plausible in performance by the snowballing pace with which the sequence is played.

But a potently constructed comic misunderstanding will supply more than just a confused respondent – it will come packed with some sort of implied debasement, as does the above exchange. Inferred by the mistake, and adding a kick to a merely silly incongruity, is Dan's apparent questioning of Kevin's manhood to which allusion has already been made.

Another common gag model defamiliarizes idiosyncrasies or shortcuts of everyday speech. At the start of *Twenty Grand*, a young man enters upon Hackett's posh, penthouse headquarters. After being made to wait for a few moments Dalton, the young man, breaks the silence: 'You wanted to see me.' Hackett responds firmly, yet evenly, as performed in the production: 'Seventeen minutes ago.' The scene continues and the men talk, maintaining a rhythmic momentum in the dialogue. While not rushed, there are no pauses for thought, little movement in the first several exchanges. The style is tautly realistic, yet pared to the bone:

> **Dalton:** I got held up.
> **Hackett:** Excuse me?
> **Dalton:** I got held up.
> **Hackett:** At gun point?
> **Dalton:** Wha'?
> **Hackett:** You got held up. Is that it?

The sequence bases itself upon a strip of everyday experience generic to contemporary urban life: someone who is late for an appointment. Most people will have been on one and probably both sides of the depicted exchange. The catch-all, exquisitely vague excuse, 'I got held up', with its variety of possible 'real' meanings, is very often allowed to slide by unchallenged. Here it is questioned and defamiliarized ('At gun point?') through a potentially 'real' exchange, for which the rather ordinary play on words receives a comic boost from the gap between a casual evasion and life-and-death crime-world jargon. The spectator might be additionally inclined to laugh out of minor relief that the sense of threat hanging over the exchange has been momentarily punctured.

Continuing in the vein of verbal patterns, there is what Nash refers to as a 'root joke' to the humour behind Hackett's patois in *Twenty Grand*. If comedy thrives on a clash of social frames, writers and performers have long put educated or 'high-class' language in the mouths of 'lower-class' characters. This strategy scores points in both directions, deflating the pretence of society's upper crust at the expense of some emblem of the 'uncultured' masses.

Very early in the play, Hackett describes a fellow criminal's encounter with a red-hot stove, 'the story of how he lost half his face'. The unfortunate man is referred to as Bozo Kearns – Bozo was the name of an American television clown and now slang for 'a stupid or insignificant person' – so any serious frame has already been knocked askew. Hackett has recounted how Bozo came home late one night, utterly exhausted, but with the intention of making himself a plate of chips. Further wearied by the peeling and chopping, he pulled a chair up to the stove to rest his head. Mistakenly, he had switched on, not the heating area under the chips, but the one under his face:

> **Hackett:** His face is on the hot side. Course he wakes up immediately, but you see, on account of Mrs Bozo constantly cookin' spice burgers and batter burgers and whatever-the-shite burgers and never cleanin' up after, Bozo's chosen super-charged heat area is mingin' with grease and gristle and muck of all sorts. Which have now attached themselves to Bozo's face. Meaning Bozo's left cheek is stuck fast to a red hot surface. Well he has to get it off the heat, and he's shriekin' like a hen night when the stripper comes on, but his face won't budge. Finally, he gives it one last almighty wrench. And his head comes up. But the left half of his face, temple to jaw, remains behind.

The story, I believe it fair to say, is disgusting. But it was delivered in performance by Carney in a histrionic, Northside Dublin dialect as if it were more an amazing curiosity, and supported by an arrangement of words that suggests a relish in the speaking. The language here is not erudite, and it is peppered with street-level crudities. But the speech is more sophisticated than one would imagine from your average ruffian, which emerges in word selection ('attached themselves'), rhythm ('grease and gristle and muck of all sorts'), figures of speech ('like a hen night when the stripper comes on') and a measured, formal shape.

This cool and eager attention to detail seeks to work upon the spectator in ironic opposition to the excruciating occurrence being described, a potentially comic eloquence and baseness interwoven. It may also be perversely entertaining to watch Hackett revel in the telling to the obvious discomfort of Dalton – as embodied by Anthony Brophy – who very obviously could not maintain his own psychic distance.

The preceding patterns show specific, identifiable templates employed by the playwright in anticipation of comic performance. Moving to a longer view of a stage world's internal structures, the 'comic pairing' represents a means for writing a basis for humorous performance into the tissue of the play. The contrasting make-ups and comic tensions between two characters becomes ready-made fodder for ongoing humour. The spectator comes to 'know' the characters and their relationship, and the astute playwright will find a way to cash in on such 'shared experience' of the characters. Indeed, the comedy team has long represented a staple of performance on the stage and in television and film.

In *Kevin's Bed* Dan and Doris, the couple whose anniversary is celebrated in each act, embody a complementary pair often found in formal comedy: a jester and authoritarian or rigid figure. Dan is a working-class postman who married 'upward' and has never been allowed to forget it by his mother-in-law; Doris is the self-proclaimed moral, spiritual, and intellectual centre of the family.

The playwright endows Dan with a position found in comedy since the slaves of Aristophanes, the plain-speaking representative from the underclasses who punctures 'civilized' pretensions. Eamon Morrissey, who was uniformly lauded by critics, played the character as an irascible working-class guy, a postman by trade, trying his best to grapple with life in the middle class.

Doris assumes the position of the rigid 'blocking' figure found in most comedies. Although drawn by Farrell and played by Barbara Brennan as a likeable enough woman, she is the character to whom all others defer. She is established early on as a defender of moral order, Brennan pursing her lips stonily at the report that her unmarried granddaughter is visibly pregnant and not at all concerned about the father's location. As is often the case with rigid figures, she has strong religious leanings – it is for such a reason that Kevin has chosen to pass off Maria, his pregnant girlfriend, as a nun come to counsel him on priesthood. The first meeting between girlfriend and mother is loaded with the spectator's knowledge that Doris breathlessly believes Maria to be a religious emissary from Rome. The charade is kept up more easily – and with various comic effects – because Maria speaks only Italian and so all translation must go through Kevin.

When Maria enters the kitchen, she excuses her intrusion in Italian, and Barbara Brennan's Doris tries to ease over any discomfort by earnestly adopting a pseudo-Italian speech pattern: 'Yes, Sister, come-a in please, there-a is something you-a want, yes?' Dan follows on with a remark intended by Eamon Morrissey's delivery to expose an ironic edge: 'Jesus, Doris, I didn't know you could speak Italian'.

It is the first in a running set of joking exchanges in which Doris clearly – and apparently without self-awareness, as played by Brennan – overclaims her ability to communicate in a foreign tongue. Dan is ever at her side, nudging her forward, while privately puncturing her pretence with a wry look toward the audience.

Where Dan as jester makes many of his jokes 'consciously', Doris as authority figure gives rise to humour beyond the character's awareness. Their comic positions can be caught in microcosm in a short exchange during the second act. Doris is put on the telephone to Maria's mother who speaks little English. In performance, Brennan warmed to the task eagerly, raising her voice and adopting an Italian cadence: 'Hello? Yes, me good too. How you? You good like me am good, yes? Me say gracias for lovely wine'.

Morrissey's Dan intervenes from the side: 'Doris, speak properly or she'll think she's talking to Tarzan'. Humour gravitates toward the human target lacking self-awareness; the jester frequently acts as conscious agent of the unmasking.

It is some matter of interest that stock comic archetypes described by Aristotle and employed by Aristophanes over 2,400 years ago can still be seen to inform characterization here at the end of the twentieth century. The *eiron*, who ironically 'dissembles his real qualities and abilities', and the *alazon*, who 'loudly lays claim to qualities and abilities not rightly his', remain key agents for humour in popular Western drama. The above comic tandem between Dan and Doris is recalled by Northrop Frye's comment:

> The multitudes of comic scenes in which one character complacently soliloquizes while another makes sarcastic asides to the audience show the contest of eiron and alazon in its purest form, and show too that the audience is sympathetic to the eiron side. (Frye, 172)

In *Twenty Grand*, a primary source of humour in the opening scene and throughout the play comes from Hackett's relationship with his son Dean, who is in his early 20s. Both men are unflinchingly violent, but Dean's feral taste for brutality, as played by Karl Shiels with an empty-headed readiness, provides a blackly comic contrast. Dean's depiction, in fact, stretches the stage world toward a broader, more traditionally comic framing. His flashy jacket and tie, caged energy and vacuousness fit within the genre, while pulling it and Hackett into a more farcically based shrewd-guy/fall-guy duo that sends up the father-son relationship.

At one point, Dean becomes confused over a newer gang-member's first name and keeps interrupting his father's high-pressure interrogation of a suspected traitor. Hackett finally attends to him, in a sense dropping out of 'professional' mode into 'paternal' mode, the sudden switch itself a stylistic cue for humour:

Hackett: Dean, d'you remember the rule?
Dean: Yes Da.
Hackett: What was the rule?

> **Dean:** If you're a thick cunt, shut up.
> **Hackett:** And what are ya, son?
> **Dean:** I'm a thick cunt, Da.
> **Hackett:** Thank you, son.

This short exchange is played quickly and clearly, like a regular father-son drill, for which the son has already realized his misstep, and demonstrates he 'knows better' in his dutiful, slightly frustrated responses. The tone, of course, is more appropriate for dealing with a child of four or five – the politeness of the phrasing and delivery is made even more incongruous by the cruel crudeness of the catechism.

A minute later, Hackett describes to the suspected traitor the instrument designed for gouging out the eyeballs of gangland turncoats:

> **Hackett:** First, this ingenious custom-made tool. Call it an eye-hook. See, it's an ordinary hunting knife, but with an inch at the point angled 90 degrees against the blade. What you do is, slip the tip into the side of the eye, fold the handle back until the hook sits snug in the socket, just behind the eyeball ... it's a bit like shuckin' an oyster ... tug firmly and Pop! Repeat on the other side and Here Comes the Night ... da da-da daa da ... Dean devised this little instrument, didn't ya Dino?
> **Dean:** Yes Da.

Hackett's speech juxtaposes the frame of gangland torture with that of a glib lecturer or a television advertisement for some amazing new kitchen gadget. Dean, rather than launching into his own explanation, again assumes the frame of schoolboy, proudly having his science project touted by Dad. Contrapuntal to the potential for witty badinage, humour loves to cut through verbal veneer.

As suggested above, the playwright can take advantage of a comic relationship built over the course of a play by reversing it. The plot has been driven by a missing £20,000, which no one will admit to having taken. Considerable violence, vividly portrayed or described, has already resulted from various efforts to recover it. With two bodies already lying about the stage and another imminent, Dean suddenly admits to having taken the money:

> **Dean:** I was gettin' a bit pissed off everyone goin' on how fuckin' smart Tommy [Dalton] was, with his credit card this an' his

computer that. Thought to meself, Dean's not as thick as everyone thinks. Dean can do somethin' smart too.

Hackett: So what did you do, Dean?

Dean: I kidnapped the assistant manager's mother, told him I'd rape her if he didn't give me twenty grand. He got it out of some fuckin' pension fund or somethin'. Didn't think it'd cause all this bother but, eh, 'fraid to say anythin' case ... well, just in case, you know? I still have it all but...

The turn of events presents a potentially comic reversal, as Dean seems the one person least equipped intellectually to carry through such a deception. His tale about the 'assistant manager's mother' is a ludicrously unworthy explanation, delivered sheepishly by the actor. There is a beat of silence as the audience wonders what unspeakable response or paternal chastisement Hackett will bestow. He then begins to applaud, and says with disbelieving pride: 'Ah, Dean, Dino, De-an-issimo, good man. First time I've felt you're your father's son.'

This moment, which comes in the midst of a minor blood bath and at a time when the spectator is probably grateful for any spark of lightness, reverses the running gag of the relationship. It calls upon residues of all the father's comically harsh reprimands thus far, and also offers cynical irony in the variety of reprehensible 'lessons' Dean seems to have learned in finally gaining his dad's approval.

As it happens, both these plays offer examples of the playwright establishing a source of humour at the start, which later, if not completely withdrawn at least contributes to an atmosphere which does not allow for unrestrained laughter.

A motivating character for comedy in the first act of *Kevin's Bed* turns nearly villainous in the second act. A fair strain of the comedy in the first act hinges on the inability of Maria, Kevin's Italian girlfriend, to speak English.

But Maria, played by Carmen Hanlon, is no longer the source of *any* humour in Act II, set twenty-five years later. She has been stubbornly enjoying her bath, despite knowledge that Kevin's parents have arrived. When she does enter the kitchen, this time she stalks her own territory and rules it unapologetically with a sharp tongue: 'Kevin! Why is everybody in here – this is the kitchen!'

Maria now speaks English all too well, and there is no longer much 'fun' in her presence. In other stage worlds, the character might have retained a humorous potential by, for example, making the change 'too well'. But in this case Farrell opts for a more disquieting quality, which Hanlon served through a deadly serious delivery in speeches like the following: 'And Kevin, I do not like you and I do not love you and when we marry it was the greatest mistake because maybe you should be a priest or something else because you are a bad husband and a bad father and a bad friend and a bad lover ...' Any audience laughter is more likely to sound like that of uncomfortable guests witnessing a marital bust-up at a dinner party. Such a pointed withdrawal of joking intentions, in effect, reverses the charge of the performance fabric, and, when handled well by playwright and production, stands to galvanize the spectator's focus on the emotional issue at hand.

Humour all but disappears toward the end of *Twenty Grand* as the 'dead bodies' accumulate onstage. It sardonically proposes entry at one point by overstating the abject denial of feeling at work in this world, bisociated with another of the fatherly lessons which has signalled humour throughout.

Ken, one of the gang members, already sprawls dead in an armchair. Rooney, the accused traitor, had earlier sustained an offstage beating that left him lame – he sits strapped to another chair and barely alive, having been stabbed several times by Dalton. Hackett, holding a gun, appears on the verge of executing Dalton when he suddenly becomes distracted by Rooney's moans. Hackett says, 'Get rid of that noise, will ya, Dean?'

Dean eagerly picks up the baseball bat, and Hackett intervenes: 'No, no, no. Not the fuckin' baseball bat. What are we, animals? Get Ken's gun.' Dean takes the gun from Ken's jacket, cocks it and shoots Rooney in the chest. Hackett intervenes again, with a paternal tone of impatience and instruction: 'Ah, in the *head*, son. Plug him in the head.' Whereupon he dispassionately aims and shoots with a routine efficiency his body seems to know by heart.

The sequence may be seen to acquire a laughably aggressive absence of feeling in the unruffled facility with which Hackett turns from one task to the next, once again interrupting 'serious business' for another quick opportunity to impress upon his son the tricks of the trade. His mildly disgusted, 'What are we, animals?' suggests some sliding scale of ethical decency in cold-blooded murder, a juxtaposition which would impress most observers as ludicrous. The quick pacing of the scene and the sudden punctuations of the gunshots subtly contribute to humour in a sequence which in real life would be unspeakably horrifying. But the father-son interludes have by now acquired the habit of cueing a frame change, offering a second, deflating perspective which may relieve the spectator (especially) in the face of excessive cruelty. In fact, almost all the play's comedy springs from Hackett and Dean, both inherited from the genre and 'spun off' from it: Hackett's self-styled gangsterese, Dean's goggle-eyed pugnacity, and their ability to clash humorously as father and son.

Twenty Grand, then, offers a good example of a 'gangland' genre, quoted from late twentieth-century film. It is decidedly not built along generically comic lines, but avails of selected humour strategies to derive an uneasy laughter by see-sawing between the brutal and the everyday. *Kevin's Bed*, in another vein, presents itself as a modern comedy of manners. It uses stock laugh-getting strategies, while working toward some sort of 'serious' commentary about life in the middle classes.

This essay has attempted to show how two plays, produced closely together in time and place yet contrasting in subject matter and mood, display generic dramatic joking patterns foreseen by the playwright through written text. These are travelling comic mini-forms we know in our bones, and they prime our spectating apparatus more than we may realize. Similar strategies used in both plays contribute to decidedly contrasting fabrics of feeling as they mesh with the surrounding stage worlds.

Although both these plays are distinctly Irish in their contexts and languages, they would not place a burden on the receptive apparatus of any English-speaking Westerner. In fact, a non-English speaker is likely to identify joking intent throughout, by recognizing comedy's time-honoured shapes and sounds beneath the surfaces of our specific cultural trappings.

Illustration 1
The Buddhist of Castleknock, Mojisola Adebayo (Rai), left, and John Olohan (Sean).

Illustration 2

Alone It Stands, top row, Karl Quinn, Niamh McGrath, Gerry McCann; bottom row, Ciaran McMahon and Conor Delaney. *Photo: Paul McCarthy.*

Illustration 3

Caught Red Handed, from left, Ian Beattie (Watson), Richard Clements (Wayne), Dan Gordon (The Leader), and Peter Balance (Reverend McIlroy). *Photo by Phil Smyth.*

Illustration 4
The Lieutenant of Inishmore, Conor Moloney (James), hanging, and
David Wilmot (Padraic). *Photo: Malcolm Davies; copyright Shakespeare
Birthplace Trust.*

Illustration 5
Stones in His Pockets, Sean Campion (Jake Hill), left, and Conleth Hill (Charlie Conlon).
Photo by Jill Jennings.

Illustration 6
Big Maggie, Eamon Morrissey. *Photo: Paul McCarthy.*

Illustration 7
Medea, Fiona Shaw (Medea) and Chorus, at the Abbey Theatre, Dublin.
Photo by Neil Libbert.

Illustration 8
That Was Then, Marion O'Dwyer (May) and Stephen Brennan (Noel).
Photo: Paul McCarthy.

Illustration 9
Kevin's Bed, from left, Sean Rocks (John), Catherine Walsh (Betty),
Barbara Brennan (Doris), and David Parnell (Kevin). *Photo by Amelia Stein.*

Illustration 10
Twenty Grand, Liam Carney (Frank Hackett), left, and Karl Shiels
(Dean Hackett). *Photo: Amelia Stein.*

Illustration 11
Smashing Times Theatre Company drama workshop, facilitated by Paul Kennedy, back centre. *Photo by Amelia Stein.*

Illustration 12
Barabbas, the early days: from left, Raymond Keane, Mikel Murfi, and
Veronica Coburn.

Sources

Farrell, Bernard, *Kevin's Bed*, unpublished rehearsal manuscript, February 1998.

Frye, Northrop, *Anatomy of Criticism* (London: Penguin, 1990).

Hughes, Declan, *Twenty Grand*, unpublished rehearsal manuscript, January 1998.

Nash, Walter, *The Language of Humour: Style and technique in comic discourse* (London: Longman, 1985).

McLeish, Kenneth, *The Theatre of Aristophanes* (London: Thames and Hudson, 1980).

11 | Laughing Together: Community-based Theatre's Vital Sense of Humour

Mary Moynihan and Paul Kennedy

Smashing Times is a professional theatre company, which special-izes in developing theatre at a local level. The company presents both professional and community-based theatre productions, and provides expertise and training to a wide range of people and or-ganizations throughout Ireland, aiming to make theatre accessible to all.

Our work with a new group always begins with general drama workshops and as the group develops, so too does the specialized nature of the workshops. For a new group, the workshops are about developing new skills in drama and theatre, making new friends, developing a love and knowledge of theatre, accessing creativity, and recognizing that theatre belongs to everyone, with the emphasis all the time on quality and innovation. Above all else they are about having fun through a creative process. It is the 'fun' or 'comedy' element of the workshop, which helps participants to relax and let go of any inhibitions they may have. As people let go, the creative work grows. When conducting a drama workshop, we would draw on a range of theatre techniques – the two main theatre practitioners we work from would be Augusto Boal and Constantin Stanislavski.

Boal is a Brazilian theatre director, writer and theorist who aspired to a new type of theatre – one which is entertaining and fun but also useful and instructive; his methods transform theatre into a democratic arena where the spectator becomes the 'spec-actor', contributing ideas, taking over roles, using theatre to confront all forms of oppression, problems such as violence, sexual harassment, poor pay, and racism. Boal has developed a range of theatre techniques under the collective heading, *Theatre of the Oppressed*. Many of the Boal exercises we use in a drama workshop are based on children's games and are ideal for putting people at their ease – games like Cat and Mouse or Brazilian Indians, in which everybody gets the chance to be the big chief as they move through the space making rhythmical movements and sounds. Just like we did when we were children. Another great game is the Circle of Knots where the entire group literally tie themselves up into one big knot, physically interacting through howls of laughter.

We explain to the group that they may feel a bit silly at the beginning but we encourage everyone to be open to this and it is amazing how their inhibitions disappear as the laughter takes over. Exercises help people to relax and to let go of stress, and the games are ideal for breaking down barriers and accessing creativity and imagination. The laughter from the games and exercises encourages a sense of exploration and helps to bond the group. There is plenty of laughter (and the occasional tear) as the participants 'play' the games and become like children again.

Women mainly attend the workshops although men are welcome and growing in numbers. But within the community it has mainly been women who have come together to share experiences, to create and to enjoy themselves. Some women shine from the start and others open up gradually like flowers blossoming. We remember one woman who came to her first workshop with her head bent, incredibly shy and lacking in confidence. By the end of the year she was on stage performing in front of huge audiences. For her first public performance she was delighted to have her two young daughters and elderly mother sitting in the front row of the auditorium, three generations of one family all involved in the magic of theatre.

Following on from the drama workshops, Smashing Times will then facilitate a local organization, if the group wishes, to develop their own theatre performances. This happens through a process of research, workshops and devising, to create original plays that come from within the heart of a particular community; because everyone plays a part in the creative process they become very passionate about what they do. Performances to date have concerned a range of themes: friendship, love, unemployment, changing communities in the context of urban development, drug and alcohol addiction, violence against women, racism and issues of cross-community conflict, diversity and reconciliation. The themes range from the light-hearted to the very serious, but in many cases, the performances are full of humour and laughter.

Eighty-five percent of our community arts productions tend to be comedy-based. Many of the actors are performing for the first time and they can sometimes prefer comedy to serious work because the laughter from the audience gives them confidence. The audiences attending the shows would know many of the actors onstage, as they are all from the same area and would be friends, relatives or neighbours. They come to support the actors and there is a great buzz and excitement in anticipation of the show. The audience come in ready to be entertained, and they laugh as they recognize their neighbour on stage now dressed as a tramp or a lover or a policeman; they laugh together in anticipation of a show that has been created within their own community and they laugh as they recognize their own stories and real-life situations now dramatized onstage. There is a strong bond between the performers and the audience as they cheer on their neighbours, friends and relatives. This bond is a unique feature of community-based performances and you can almost see the invisible threads connecting the audience to the performers, where everyone is raised to one level and are working together.

A good example of this process can be taken from our involvement with Ringsend, where Smashing Times presented *Over the Bridge* in association with the local Watersedge Community Drama Group. Smashing Times director and writer Paul Kennedy wrote and directed *Over the Bridge,* which was first presented in the City Arts Centre, Dublin, in November 2000, as part of the Dublin Millennium celebrations, following a year of research, interviews, devising and rehearsals with people from the local community. Accompanying the performance was a photographic exhibition and a video documentary on show in the theatre foyer – all linked to the theme of Ringsend. Based on the original success of the project, Smashing Times was then invited by the Dublin Docklands Development Authority to present *Over the Bridge* as part of the Docklands Festival in June 2001.

As part of the project, local people were interviewed and asked to share stories about growing up in Ringsend. A wide range of people agreed to share their stories with us, ranging from dockers to the local barber to the people who lived in the flats on Thorncastle Street. One woman told a story from her childhood. She remembered sneaking into the morgue of St. Patrick's hospital with some other children and being fascinated by the dead bodies lying on the slabs. One day she and a few other children were kneeling down saying a prayer for the soul of the corpse, when gas was released from the dead body. The children were terrified at the noise and ran out of the morgue and on to the street and over the bridge back to Ringsend. This story was included in the play, *Over The Bridge*, in dramatic form.

Stella Gaffney from Ringsend was the woman who told this story, and on the opening night of the play in the City Arts Centre she arrived with family and friends and sat in a seat in the front row. You could hear her laughter at the back of the theatre when this scene was acted out on stage. What was she laughing at? What was the audience laughing at? Her laughter was intimately connected to her childhood memories – and these memories were all the more poignant because her story was being acted out in public. She was now sharing her story with the audience. And yet in some real way, she *is* the author, the originator of the story. Stella spoke to us afterwards and found the experience immensely rewarding and entertaining. What was the audience laughing at? Community arts plays are for local audiences. This does not diminish their impact. It creates circumstances where the audience and actors can share in a common understanding of oral and local history. The audience responded with laughter to Stella's story because it rang true to them, because they recognized the place names mentioned in the story, and also because they knew that all the stories in that particular play had been researched and collected from local people. This shared laughter is in some ways reminiscent of the way families or extended families share stories. Things can be funny because they belong to our collective memory as a group. We laugh to reinforce our communal identity.

Many of the communities that Smashing Times work with have experienced poverty and varying levels of disadvantage, yet they still share a strong sense of community and a strong sense of culture. Many of the performances become a celebration by a group, using the creative process to celebrate their own stories and unique cultural experiences, in addition to celebrating the sense of achievement that comes from creating and presenting one's own show. In community theatre practice, both the participants and audience come to the theatre to celebrate, which is why laughter and humour come to play an important role.

This combination of comedy and celebration was evident in *Over the Bridge*. Paul recalls that when he was interviewing the elderly people of Ringsend, nearly all the stories they told him had a comic element. Even hardship stories about growing up had a funny twist, and the director believes this is because people in poorer areas used humour in their everyday lives to alleviate hardship. Comedy and humour had served a real and practical function in their lives, helping them to survive times of austerity. As an audience this makes them particularly receptive to comic moments onstage. Some audiences will even laugh at tragic moments, *not* out of disrespect, but out of the habit of laughter. Tragic moments in their own lives are interspersed with laughter and an instinctive reaction to tragedy in the theatre can also produce laughter.

Community theatre audiences laugh more easily and openly and in some ways more sincerely than audiences in the 'mainstream' theatre, because they do not enter a theatre space with received notions about the 'sanctity of art'. They are to a certain extent a very relaxed, yet spontaneous audience, by which we mean they bring a fresh eye and a fresh ear, because in most cases they would not be conditioned to react like audiences at the larger theatres such as the Gate or the Abbey. They also cry and share an empathy that reaches through everyone when tragic moments are presented, particularly when the issues are very real and close to home: a child dying from a drugs overdose, the realities of life in war-torn Belfast, or the senseless and violent rape of a woman. But the comedy always comes back, because in a way it has to. One example of this is when we staged *Where have all the spoons gone?*, also in Ringsend in 1999.

Where have all the spoons gone? was written by a local woman, Tara Grey, from a devising process conducted by Paul Kennedy. It dealt with the childhood and adolescent experiences of a drug addict. A lot of the content of the play contained quite harrowing scenes – drug overdoses, distraught parents, communities in crisis, failed attempts at rehabilitation culminating in the death of the main character at the end of the play. Yet when the play was first performed in Ringsend (as part of the National Drug Awareness Week), there was a strangely electric buzz in the audience. Some people in the audience seemed to laugh at inappropriate moments, when great suffering was being portrayed by the actors. What were they laughing at? Was it derisive laughter? The play received a standing ovation. And again at the next night's performance … more laughter. Why? Well, because it seemed that the audience laughed at moments of *recognition*. The laughter was saying, 'I know exactly where you're coming from', or, 'I've been there, and it's funny now to see that experience represented on the stage by people from my community'. The laughter is also, importantly, the community's way of saying to the actors, 'We're here, we're listening, we think you're great to get up there on the stage and perform for us'. It is a part of the community, it is a part of survival, and it brings people closer together and is, of course, an expression of enjoyment.

Devised performances enable groups to explore issues relevant to their lives, whether they are personal, social or political. Another play titled *The Winter of My Soul* was developed from a programme of workshops run by Smashing Times with the North West Inner City Women's Network based in the Smithfield/Markets area of Dublin. *The Winter of My Soul* was scripted by Ann O'Rourke, a local woman, from a devising process conducted by drama facilitator and director Mary Moynihan, and is based on an actual event from Ann's life. When in her twenties and with a small child, Ann had an operation to remove a brain tumour. A month after the operation she was at home and received a letter to attend the hospital immediately for further tests. Something had gone wrong.

The play opens with the central character, called Ann, reading the letter and anxiously making arrangements to go back to hospital. Ann sets off to the Richmond, a hospital that specialized in head injuries and was, at that time, based in the inner-city area of Dublin. The hospital was situated next to a hostel called the Morning Star Hostel for homeless men. Ann is admitted to a ward with three other very ill people; we witness her fear and confusion at what is happening, and the different patients and nurses she meets as she waits for a doctor to come and counsel her. As she waits, her anxieties increase. When a doctor finally arrives in the ward, Ann thinks she has lost her reason, as the doctor (or the person she thinks is the doctor) proceeds to do a comedy routine of song and dance for each of the patients, including those who are comatose. Through a series of almost surreal scenes, Ann witnesses in growing disbelief the doctor singing and dancing for each of his patients, as he encourages them all to keep up their spirits. Ann believes that the brain tumour has caused her to go mad, and it is only when she realizes that the 'doctor' is an impostor, a homeless man who is a regular intruder into the hospital from the Morning Star Hostel next door, that she sees the funny side of things and breaks into laughter. Ann eventually overcomes her illness and there is a suggestion that her willingness to laugh at life in all its absurdities has helped her to survive an emotional and frightening experience.

As a comedy, *The Winter of My Soul* brought forth howls of laughter from the audience. Again there was that strong sense of support from the audience as they laughed at the comedy in the play, and as a way of encouraging their family and friends on stage. Local women performed the play and many of them brought an inventiveness and originality to the work, which was exciting to watch. The script started from an original story, further developed through a series of improvisations in which each of the women evolved her own character. Because each actor had created the character she was playing, there was a heightened sense of truth, and it was the women themselves who created the comedy on stage as they infused their own personalities and senses of humour into the performance.

The arts can help us to define a sense of ourselves within society and help us to explore and express our cultural identities. Both professional and community theatre practices can be used to help a community define itself, but, of equal importance, to help a community re-invent itself. I am referring to the notion of change, using theatre to encourage change for a better and more inclusive society. Increasingly, Smashing Times is using theatre to explore social and political issues, using theatre to support cultures and giving those voices a form through which they can be heard. A recent production, *A Chain of Hands,* is a performance piece that raises awareness of racism and celebrates cultural diversity. Mary Moynihan scripted and directed the play following a workshop and devising process run in association with the North West Inner City Women's Network, Prussia Street Women's Group, and the Vincentian Refugee Centre, all based in Dublin. It was presented in March 2002 at various community venues to celebrate Anti-Racism Day and has since gone on tour. The show was performed by participants from black and minority ethnic communities, working alongside professional actors and participants from community-based drama organizations. As part of the workshop and devising process, participants from many different backgrounds came together to explore issues of racism through the medium of drama.

In the final script the stories and experiences of refugees and asylum seekers coming to Ireland were brought to life onstage to raise awareness of racism. A number of scenes contained depictions of the harrowing experiences endured by some refugees, yet comedy also played an important role in the production, allowing for a more subtle absorption of the serious message contained within the play.

In Ireland today there are a lot of exaggerated and alarmist comments being made about the number of asylum seekers coming to Ireland in recent years. There are also many rumours in circulation about the types of benefits to which asylum seekers are entitled. *A Chain of Hands* uses comedy to show how many of these rumours have been blown completely out of proportion, particularly by the media, and how the rumours are contributing to negative stereotyping. Siobhán, a central character in the play, is fearful of the many new communities being 'dumped', as she sees it, into her area, which is already under pressure from problems such as drugs, high unemployment, and a lack of access to education and other facilities. She meets up with a journalist, a crazy, over-the-top character who bounds on stage at every opportunity to report in a frenzied manner on how, 'the floodgates are opening as a new army of poor march through the country'. Egged on by the journalist, Sheila tells the audience that, 'there's a black family up our road keeping live snakes in their bath...to drink the blood, and if those snakes escape they'll poison us all'. Sheila and the journalist compete with each other as to who has the wildest story, which the journalist then proceeds to broadcast as 'news', until he is finally led off foaming at the mouth and babbling about 'alien invaders' and 'spaceships from Mars'. Sheila believes the misinformation and wonders whether the recent floods experienced by the country are due to the number of asylum seekers. She exclaims, 'Oh God, maybe the country's sinking under their weight!'

The comedy in *A Chain of Hands* is important for holding the audience's attention and for putting across a serious message in a way that is engaging and non-threatening. Theatre is a medium that is accessible to everybody and provides a creative and enter-taining format for stimulating public awareness of issues such as racism. The issues become more real and engaging because they are presented in human terms through characters and storylines. Comedy allows the script to promote cultural diversity as a value in our society without being too didactic or preachy, and the audience's response to the play is hopefully stronger as they are more open to what the play is saying.

A Chain of Hands confronted people on the subject of their perceptions of asylum seekers and refugees, and told some of the personal and tragic stories behind the statistics. The play presented the personal experiences of refugees and also the experiences and fears of Irish people engaging with new communities in Ireland. Despite the sometimes tragic content of the play, there was laughter in the audience. In the play Katyia, a refugee from Kosovo has asked to join the local woman's group. She is refused by Siobhan who explains that, 'it took us a long time to get this group together, we really don't want their kind here'. She then leans over and politely pats the refugee's hand saying in her friendliest voice, 'no offence missus', which, at every performance, produced laughter from the audience. Is this the laughter of recognition, particularly when people were recognizing their own prejudices? Possibly, the laughter is an admittance of guilt: 'Yes, I am like that sometimes'. The recognition here is really important, but it is the laughter that gives it expression – not glib laughter, but genuine laughter, which suggests the possibility of change. While presenting stories of pain and tragedy, the play used comedy as a tool to bring about change, challenging people to change their habitual way of perceiving the world. In this sense, comedy is important for tackling core issues within any community, particularly when using a comedy that is rooted in the community's identity, but also looking ahead to ask in what ways the community needs to change.

Because comedy plays such an important role in community theatre, it is important to ask, does comedy allow a community to *avoid* facing up to certain issues? The answer is 'sometimes' – because comedy can also be a way to mask over and refuse to deal with painful areas. While being funny is definitely important in its own right, comedy and community theatre should not be merely a palliative; it ultimately has to have some other function than to be funny. This can be developed over a period of time, which again emphasizes the importance of long-term access to the arts at a local level.

The work of Smashing Times, particularly the collaborative approach, encourages people to become the creators of their own work, to develop their own talents and to use the power of drama for their own benefit. Community theatre is by its nature socially conscious and while a professional artist and group may not begin with a political agenda, it is important not to shy away from such issues as they arise – and central to this can be the use of different styles and forms of comedy. We also believe that the use of different forms of comedy should be explored further within community theatre, for example developing within a community context the skills for clowning, *commedia dell'arte* or mime, forms which are often underutilized within community theatre practice.

The activities and benefits of the theatre work practised by Smashing Times are wide and varied, but it is interesting that at all levels, whether in a drama workshop to develop specific skills, in a devising workshop for script development or during performance, alongside the passion and dedication there is always the element of fun and enjoyment. There are those who may believe that only the rare few are true artists. In Smashing Times we believe that everyone has creative potential. There is a huge amount of creativity out there and Smashing Times will continue to act as the facilitators, taking part in a whole new growth in theatre that is both exciting and challenging.

In Smashing Times we use theatre to entertain, to foster creativity, to stimulate awareness and to bring about action and change in a creative way. Humour is one of many elements used within our work to entertain and to bring people together. Humour is also used as a political tool to encourage change in a creative way where, together, we as practitioners and participants are sharing laughter (and tears) to define our experiences as they are and also as we would like them to be.

12 | Macabre Merriment in McDonagh's Melodrama, The Beauty Queen of Leenane

Rebecca Wilson

In the common perception of melodrama as sensational, emotionally hyperbolic theatre, the comic dimension is often neglected. Yet the comic element is as integral to the basic formula as are the villain, the hero and the heroine. Initially, in traditional melodrama, comedy was located in a benevolent clown figure, virtue in the hero and heroine, and evil in the villain. As this mutable form developed, characterization became less rigid and character traits merged and/or overlapped, giving rise to 'villains who were more to be pitied than censured',[1] flawed heroes and heroines, and comedy that no longer centred in a benevolent clown. John McCormick notes that:

> As a greater psychological element crept in, and as the clear distinctions between good and evil, which has been so much a hallmark of the genre, were increasingly eroded...audiences were expected to 'understand' the villain rather than conspue [sic] him.[2]

In Martin McDonagh's melodrama, *The Beauty Queen of Leenane*, first performed at the Town Hall Theatre Galway on 1 February, 1996, we have victim-villains as protagonists, and comedy, rather

---

[1] Frank Rahill, *The World of Melodrama*. (Pennsylvania State: University Press, 1967), p.xv.

[2] John McCormick, 'Origins of Melodrama' in *Prompts 6*. (*Irish Theatre Archives*, Sept. 1983), pp.5-12 (p.12).

than residing in a comic characterization, is the woof in the warp of McDonagh's melodramatic dramaturgy; it is this comic weft that this paper is concerned with. In the words of Charles Spencer, this play is 'wildly funny, deeply affecting and generally macabre, all at the same time',[3] and these other moods must also be touched upon in order to contextualize the comic element, particularly since the comedy here does not at all offer comic relief, but rather intensifies the pain; it is the lightning flash that illuminates and etches the tragic moment.

McDonagh both upholds and inverts the tenets of traditional melodrama in this play which, in its Irish localization, is redolent of a Syngean aesthetic, and is universal in its depiction of human pain, loss and absurdity. Here is a landscape painted by Francis Bacon. This is rustic Ireland, but the poetic, bitterly romantic terrain of Synge and the idyllic picturesque pastoral land of Boucicault have been flayed away to expose a bleak 'big ould hill', steep, muddy and rocky that, without a car, can only be reached by 'wading through all that skitter'. Here, incidentally, we see an inversion of a fairy-tale trope in melodrama: in a tower on top of a mountain, incarcerated by an ogress-cum-wicked witch, the virgin heroine, albeit a 40-year-old resentful, frustrated and repressed virgin, waits for a lover-saviour. The lover-saviour, after braving 'all that skitter' rather than an enchanted forest, proves impotent to deliver her from the ogress. But then what can the heroine be but an ogress herself, since one ogress can only beget another?

Mother, Mag, and daughter, Maureen, live in mutually destructive symbiosis in a dreary village in the west of Ireland. Mag is dependent, selfish, demanding, manipulative; Maureen is mentally fragile, frustrated, trapped. At a neighbour's party, Maureen renews her acquaintance with Pato, a man near her own age who works in England, leading to mutual attraction and an unconsummated one-night stand. Mag attempts to destroy the budding relationship. Pato returns to England but writes to Maureen, asking her to go to America with him. Mag intercepts and burns the letter, but when Maureen later taunts her with the sexual exploit that in fact never

---

[3] Charles Spencer reviewing 'The Beauty Queen of Leenane' in *The Daily Telegraph*, 8 March 1996.

happened, Mag inadvertently lets slip comments that arouse Maureen's suspicions. Under torture by Maureen scalding her with boiling oil, Mag confesses to the knowledge of the letter and reveals its contents. This precipitates Maureen's murder of Mag and descent into madness. In the final scene we learn that Pato went off to America believing that Maureen did not want to see him. Pato's brother, Ray, tells her that Pato is engaged to a girl in America and Maureen, the 'beauty queen of Leenane', succumbs to the madness that was always hovering around her.

Mag and Maureen do not represent an idealized, sentimentalized mother-and-child relationship; they are two unhappy, malignant harpies tearing and empoisoning each other. Into this nest of vipers comes the stranger, Pato, neither romanticized man of mystery nor villain, but a normal, ordinary man who, unwittingly, is the catalyst that will ignite the catastrophe. Here is an astringent inversion of a formulaic melodramatic structure: instead of the villain despoiling the place of innocence and activating the plot, the potential hero enters a vile place and activates the plot. There is also the reverse, absolute adherence to the moral principles (the 'moral occult') of melodrama: because she has tortured and killed, Maureen cannot be saved. The ordinary, normal, innocent man offers Maureen escape and a normal, ordinary life which the ethics of the 'moral occult' must perforce deny her. And throughout this baleful tale, comedy glitters wickedly.

McDonagh has intermeshed: a double-edged, interlocked retention and inversion of much ideology, iconography and topography of 'classic' melodrama; thematics of Gothic melodrama flavoured with elements of Grand Guignol; a macabre 'gallows humour' and streaks of lasciviousness recalling those lode veins of the Irish comic tradition delineated by Vivian Mercier in *The Irish Comic Tradition*; comedy carried by the protagonists (or rather antagonists) rather than clown figures; and damaged victim-villains, 'injured scoundrels', rather than a villain figure serving as a cipher of evil. Thus, instead of a fleshly embodiment of evil, there is 'a disembodied presence of evil', here allegorized by the foul-smelling kitchen – a hell's kitchen indeed.

The set of the *Beauty Queen* is the typical country-cottage kitchen of much Irish melodrama (or Eamon de Valera's bucolic fantasy) but this kitchen is no fragrant hearthstone of nurture and nourishment, nor is it the impersonal space of, for example, McGahern's *The Power of Darkness* (1991), where evil is plotted, nor D'Alton's *Lovers Meeting* (1941), where old sins fester, nor Keane's *Sive* (1959), where greed sacrifices innocence. These are neutral rooms, innocent in themselves of the human malevolence and/or mischance breeding in them. Disease and evil are palpable in the *Beauty Queen's* kitchen, which stinks of the diseased urine that Mag, suffering from a urine infection, pours down the sink. This kitchen is a fetid miasma of unwholesomeness, as warped as the symbiotically empoisoned mother and daughter who inhabit it; it signifies 'evil as a real, irreducible force'.[4] Yet it is also a fount of humour, a powerful, dicephalous dramatic device engendering both comedy and revulsion. The revulsion caused by the stench (effectively projected in performance by a grimace or a shudder) of diseased urine is comically leavened by Mag pouring a potty of 'wee' down the sink and 'wee' down the kitchen sink gives rise to several episodes of comedy, verbal and visual. The following exchange is one of the funniest episodes in the play:

> **Ray:** This house does smell of pee, this house does.
> **Mag:** (*Pause. Embarrassed*): Em, cats do get in.
> **Ray:** Do cats get in?
> **Mag:** They do. (*Pause*) They do go to the sink.
> **Ray:** (*Pause*): What do they go to the sink for?
> **Mag:** To wee.
> **Ray:** To wee? They go to the sink to wee? (*Piss-taking.*)
> [McDonagh seems to be enjoying a pun here]: Sure, that's mighty good of them. You do get a very considerate breed of cat up this way so.
> **Mag:** (*Pause*): I don't know what breed they are. (McDonagh, 40-41)

The verbal comedy is self-explanatory and, punctuated by the pauses accentuating the contrasting moods of preposterous dissembling, discomfiture, mild bewilderment and sarcasm, give ample room for expressive visual performance comedy.

---

4 Peter Brooks, *The Melodramatic Imagination* (Yale: University Press, 1995), p.13.

The putrid sink gives rise to somewhat more uncomfortable comedy in the scene in which Maureen, after offering Pato a mug of tea, drags him over to 'smell that sink', upon which *Pato leans into the sink, sniffs it, then pulls his head away in disgust* (McDonagh, 28). This is a facial gesture which is bound to raise a laugh, albeit a squeamish one, which is rather in keeping with Pato *'sipping'* his tea *'squeamishly'* (McDonagh, 29), another facial gesture which often arouses laughter in an audience. The entire vista is a horrid and hilarious melee of Mag demanding attention for her 'scoulded hand' and deploring all mention of 'wee', Maureen complaining that she has to wash her 'praities' in an unhygienic sink while serving Pato tea, and Pato trapped in embarrassment and too polite to refuse the tea. Indeed, the incompatible juxtaposition of disgust and gustatory hospitality – 'And doesn't even rinse it either. Now is that hygienic? And she does have urine infection too, is even less hygienic. I wash me praities in there. Here's your tea now, Pato' – is an ingeniously funny and disturbing construct. The incongruity of the situation supplies the comedy, provoking an effect somewhat akin to the Freudian theory of 'humorous displacement ... a means of withdrawing energy from the means of unpleasure that is already in preparation and transforming it by discharge into pleasure'. This scene borders on farce. The scene hurtles toward psychic violence and culminates in bitter bathos. Like all intensely narcissistic creatures, Mag is oblivious to anyone else. Treachery is a staple of melodrama. McDonagh interweaves both these factors in this astonishing scene of terrible pathos and cruel comedy, which builds to Mag, viciously and exultingly, telling Pato of Maureen's stay in a mental hospital. Mother and daughter shout at each other with mounting, venomous aggression, Pato steps between them, Mag exits to get Maureen's hospitalization papers, Maureen sadly confesses her mental instability and Pato tries to comfort her, Mag returns triumphantly brandishing the papers, Pato leaves, promising to write and Maureen, crouching on the floor, hugging her new dress that Mag has thrown in a corner, is as shattered as if Mag has taken a club to her. After the medley of frenetic stage business Maureen exits, an image of heart-rending despair. Nothing is funny any more. Then Mag, utterly indifferent to the devastation she has caused, sticks her finger in her porridge and, horrifically and comically, complains, twice, that her 'porridge has gone cold now' (McDonagh, 34). The effect on an audience must be to produce a laugh, a Beckettian 'dianoetic laugh' that laughs at that which is not happy.[5]

Porridge – Complan – cod-in-butter-sauce – shortbread fingers – Mag's world revolves around food. Typical of the infant personality craving constant feeding, Mag is obsessed with being fed. Food is a recognized signifier of need and comfort, the primary demand of the infant for its survival, the centre of its world, and of Mag's. A rare excursion into town is looked forward to less for the outing than for the possibility of getting shortbread fingers. Food provides the axle for a scene that, ingeniously and comically, expresses a complex psychological nexus of narcissistic self-absorption and infantile demands for nurturing. Ray, waiting to give Pato's letter to the absent Maureen, is getting more and more impatient. Mag wants him to go before Maureen can get the letter, urging him, 'Be off and give your letter to me...I'll make sure she gets it' (McDonagh, 38) and insinuating that Maureen may not be back until morning. Yet her need for nurturing pulls her the other way as, totally oblivious to Ray's irritation, she asks him to make her 'a mug of tea ... Or a mug of Complan ... Or a Cup-a-Soup do me'(McDonagh, 41). The incongruity of conflicting moods and desires, including the pitted stubbornness of fixated age versus restless youth, furnishes an acerbic comedy.

Prophetic violence lurks in the comedy of Ray's yearning for the women's 'great oul poker', with which he could 'take out a half a dozen coppers ... just for the fun of seeing the blood running out of them' (McDonagh, 39). There is a sinister dramatic pro-lepsis in Ray's comic fantasy of battering coppers with the poker and seeing bloody gouts, since Mag is later in fact bloodily battered with the selfsame poker. Ironically Mag, by refusing to sell Ray the poker, is retaining the instrument of her murder. In terms of performance, Ray's *wielding the poker* (McDonagh, 39) suggests a comic orgy of mimed violence reminiscent of the frenetic film clown, Jimmy Finlayson, of the old Hal Roach comedies. Aggression is common to comedy and staged violence is often,

---

[5] Vivian Mercier, *The Irish Comic Tradition*. See Chapters Two and Three.

though by no means always, risible; the motives for our laughter are complex and seem to be partly impelled by context and degrees of identification. For example, we laugh as Punch clobbers Judy and the policeman and throws his baby out of a window, although domestic and civic violence and infanticide are not laughing matters. (Our glee as he hangs the hangman and cheats the devil is straightforward, self-explanatory recoiling from mortality.) We do not at all laugh at the Carney brothers' violence in Tom Murphy's *A Whistle in the Dark*, but can barely stop laughing as brothers Valene and Coleman consistently batter each other in McDonagh's *The Lonesome West*. Laughter provoked by theatrical violence seems to be contingent on context, treatment and style rather than content.

To return briefly to the poker: in the last scene Ray, unaware that Maureen has murdered Mag with the poker, still covets it. As Vivian Mercier has so diligently traced, 'gallows humour' has long featured in Irish culture and the poker provides a conduit for this when Ray's bargaining ('A fiver I'll give you … G'wan. Six!') (McDonagh, 58-9), for that 'awful good poker' is refused by Maureen's, 'No. It does have sentimental value for me' (McDonagh, 58-9). From a performance viewpoint, Ray unknowingly handling the poker while countering Maureen's assertion that drugs are dangerous with, 'Maybe they are, maybe they are. But there are plenty of other things just as dangerous, would kill you just as easy. Maybe even easier' (McDonagh, 54) would certainly present grimly comic dramatic irony.

Comedy and suspense, both staple ingredients of melodrama, revolve around that archetypal generic device, the letter. The letter or document is a standard, crucial iconic device of melodrama, sometimes to detonate the catastrophe, at other times as a sort of *deus ex machina* to resolve it. McDonagh uses Pato's letter to precipitate disaster, but with an ironic bitter twist that accentuates the pain. Had Pato's letter reached Maureen, she could have escaped; that chance was stolen from her by Mag stealing the letter, by archetypal melodramatic treacherous villainy. This sets in motion the chain of events that ultimately entraps Maureen; thus, ironically, the potential key to her liberation is the key that locks her finally in her prison, as McDonagh offers us four iconic ingredients of traditional melodrama: secretive treachery, the letter, the oath and the thwarted escape, as well as comic instances laced throughout the scene. The spectators may ultimately be left with the bitter aftertaste of John Greenleaf Whittier's couplet:

> For of all sad words of tongue or pen
> The saddest are these: it might have been!

But they may well giggle – or guffaw – while holding their breath in suspense when Ray, breaking his word to Pato, leaves the letter with Mag, making her swear not to open it: 'And may God strike you dead if you do open it?' She responds with, 'And may God strike me dead if I do open it, only he'll have no need to strike me dead because I won't be opening it' (McDonagh, 41). The ludicrousness of the childish oath, recalling playground oaths of 'swear to God and hope to die' and Mag's barefaced lie supply a verbal comedy which suitable gesture and vocal tone may reinforce; Ray's indecisive stage business with the letter, repeatedly putting it down and picking it up, and Mag's stealthy moves towards the letter, to be unwittingly truncated, with the meticulous timing of farce by Ray, present a well-worn but nonetheless always-effective visual motif of comic suspense. Also in keeping with patterns of time-tested comic exits, Ray goes out the door but does not leave. Mag starts out of the rocking chair then, remembering she hasn't heard Ray's footsteps, she 'sits back serenely'. The door bursts open, Ray sticks his head in, Mag 'smiles at him innocently' and Ray exits. It might be a cliché but it works. Then all comedy stops as Mag reads the letter and burns it.

As is typical of this play, the comedy is not presented in set pieces but is interleaved within the melodramatic plot and process. Consider, for example, the comic oath and Mag's murderous end. Gothic poetic justice and the 'moral occult' of 'classic' melodrama, Peter Brooks's theories of a morally based ideological apparatus that supplanted notions of divinely ordained justice, can be perceived in Mag's nemesis. Mag has broken a vow, one of melodrama's sacrosanct icons. (Ray did not do as Pato asked, but Ray never promised anything, let alone take an oath.) Not only has she sworn dishonestly, she has dishonestly invoked the Sacred. She does open the letter and she is struck dead, not by God but by

Maureen. Thus Mag's retribution is not numinous, it can be rationally explained by Maureen's rage, yet a Gothic reverberation is unmistakeable in the manner of her death. However, the instrument of her nemesis is not some metaphysical phenomenon but a corporeal fury. All this accords with Brooks' stance (in reference to the 'moral occult') that, 'in the absence of a true Sacred ...what is most important in a man's life is his ethical drama and the ethical implications of his psychic drama'.[6] Thus McDonagh, within a melodramatic frame, has interwoven elements of the serious and the merry play.

Licentious humour, like macabre and gallows humour, with roots in Irish myth and legend, introduces episodes which tumble into pain and dismay. In the already mentioned Scene IV, the morning after Pato has stayed overnight, Maureen comes out in bra and slip, flaunting sexuality and, much to Pato's embarrassment, sits across his lap (her state of undress and exhibitionism recalling a lap-dancer), kissing him and taunting Mag with licentious remarks. Her, 'We was careful, weren't we, Pato? Careful enough, cos we don't need any babies coming, do we? We do have enough babies in this house to be going on with', (McDonagh, 27) uses sexual innuendo, always sure to raise a titter, to torment Mag with both the notion of active sexuality and the reversed situation of child-as-carer and mother as child-cum-tyrant, the situation which imprisons and embitters Maureen. The innuendo accelerates into blunt licentiousness – rude, crude and sure to bring the house down with laughter:

> **Maureen:** (*To Pato*): You'll have to be putting that thing of yours in me again before too long is past, Pato. I do have a taste for it now, I do...
> **Pato:** *Maureen...*
> **Maureen:** A mighty oul taste. Uh-huh.
> *Pato gets up and idles around in embarrassment.* (McDonagh, 28)

Mercier suggests laughter at licentiousness could be prompted by the 'excessive and absurd',[7] here typified by Maureen's be-

---

[6] Peter Brooks, *The Melodramatic Imagination*, p.52.
[7] Mercier, p.49.

haviour, and also by its function as a release of sexual repression. Mercier's observations could well apply to this scene.

Maureen's narcissistic need to irritate Mag totally ignores Pato's discomfiture; the poisonous relationship with Mag of hate and spite overrides any constructive feeling for Pato. Her self-destructive goading of Mag provokes Mag's vicious, treacherous retaliation: the insistent divulging of Maureen's stay in a mental hospital. Then the scene tilts: Maureen's state of undress, at first intentionally sexually provocative, now exposes her helplessness; what had begun as a brazen sexual ploy transmutes into naked vulnerability. She descends into a slough of self-pity as she relays her status as victim, victim of racism in England, victim of mental instability, victim of her mother in Ireland. Her abysmal lack of self-esteem misconstrues Pato's suggestion that she put some clothes on as revulsion and rejection.

Shamed by her 'doolally' (McDonagh, 30) breakdown, shamed by her assumption of Pato's rejection, and, in line with the melo-dramatic process through the centuries, this pathetic, broken figure is very likely to arouse pity in the spectator, a pity intensified by contrast with the earlier 'excessive and absurd' brazen hussy, as lewd comedy transmutes into naked despair.

A similar schema can be seen in Scene VIII. The scene opens with a sexually charged duel, fraught with mother-daughter sexual antagonism: Maureen licentiously bragging about her fictitious sexual experience and taunting Mag as being 'past it', and Mag smugly sneering with her knowledge that there was no sexual adventure – Pato was too drunk to perform sexually and Maureen is as virginal as ever. Maureen's lewd braggadocio gives the hos-tility a comic dimension; witness Maureen playing on Mag's obsessive craving for food as food for lascivious language and gesture:

> **Maureen:** Do you want a shortbread finger?
> **Mag:** I do want a shortbread finger.
> **Maureen:** Please.
> **Mag:** Please.
> *Maureen gives Mag shortbread finger, after waving it phallically in the air a moment.*
> **Maureen:** Remind me of something, shortbread fingers do.

Mag: I suppose they do now.
Maureen: I suppose it's so long since you've seen what they remind me of, you do forget what they look like. (McDonagh, 45-6)

Again lewd and crude, plangent with gesturement and certain to raise convulsive laughter. (In a local performance in Westport the actress stroked, sucked and nibbled another shortbread finger and the hall shook with laughter; vulgar comedy, absolutely, but so, reportedly, was *komos,* although the *Beauty Queen* ends not with marriage but living entombment.) Then the scene tilts as Maureen suspects that Mag is withholding information about Pato, and an episode that started with sexual braggadocio transmogrifies into sadism with the torture of Mag; again an episode that started with lascivious comedy ends in brutal despair, this time Mag's as, tortured and abandoned, she quietly intones, 'But who'll look after me, so?' (McDonagh, 49)

Maureen's torture of Mag, a harrowing scene steeped in the horror of Grand Guignol, is a cardinal scene in the play, and thus, I feel, merits further comment. This may seem a digression from the main thrust of this article, but since agony, horror and humour are as symbiotically inextricable in this play as the protagonists, further commentary seems called for, especially as the torture seems to have a sexual motivation and so is linked to the earlier comic lascivious bravado (which in itself carries a bitter irony, since it pretends to celebrate a non-event). Maureen's scalding of Mag's previously scalded hand with boiling oil seems to be motivated by her desire to extract information about Pato. But the ritualistic procedure, the donning of the rubber gloves, the turning up of the radio to drown Mag's screams, the patient waiting for the oil to boil and the excruciating, intense brutality of the act, '*Maureen slowly and deliberately takes her mother's shrivelled hand, holds it down on the burning range, and. starts slowly pouring some of the hot oil over it*' (McDonagh, 47), suggests a sadism that has little to do with pressuring for information. Also, Mag's terror at the ritualistic preparations before the oil has been near her suggests a repeat performance, something which Mag claims has indeed happened. The preparations are enough to make Mag confess to having intercepted Pato's letter and read it; it is after that confession that Maureen actually starts to pour the hot oil over Mag's hand. After

Mag admits to having burnt the letter and reveals its contents, (Pato's apology for being too drunk to perform sexually and his offer to take Maureen to America), Maureen throws '*the considerable remainder of the oil*' (McDonagh, 48) over her, an act of pure sadistic hate, since she now has the information. Given Maureen's sexual repression, which is such a fundamental feature of the play, and the sexually loaded context of the scene, it can only be assumed that, along with the hatred fanned by vengeance, that last splurge of hot oil is a sadistic act charged with sadism's inherent sexuality. Also, a cruel parallelism can be discerned in the burning of the letter and the burning of the hand.

Macabre humour opens and closes this play; in the first scene it hinges on a grimly amusing fantasy, 'excessive and absurd'; in the last it is funny and harrowing, a comedy that highlights misery, a reification of the comic instant that illuminates the tragic moment. The earlier comic episode opens with Mag's Agony Aunt-like advice not to speak to strangers, accelerates into the macabre-grotesque with Maureen's gleeful (and proleptic) fantasy of clobbering Mag and is abruptly – and comically - terminated by Mag's narcissistic demands for feeding:

> **Mag:** … Although some people it would better not to say hello to. The fella up and murdered the poor oul woman in Dublin and he didn't even know her. The news that story was on, did you hear of it? Strangled, and didn't even know her. That's a fella it would be better not to talk to. That's a fella it would be better to avoid outright. [Ironically, Mag is talking to her murderer]
>
> *Maureen brings Mag her tea, then sits at the table.*
>
> **Maureen:** Sure, that sounds exactly the type of fella I would like to meet, and then bring him home to meet you, if he likes murdering oul women.
> **Mag:** That's not a nice thing to say, Maureen.
> **Maureen:** Is it not, now?
> **Mag:** (*Pause*) Sure why would he be coming all this way out from Dublin? He'd just be going out of his way.
> **Maureen:** For the pleasure of me company he'd come. Killing you, it'd just be a bonus for him.
> **Mag:** Killing you I bet he first would be.
> **Maureen:** I could live with that so long as I was sure he'd be clobbering you soon after. If he clobbered you with a big axe or

something and took your oul head off and spat in your neck, I wouldn't mind at all, going first. Oh no, I'd enjoy it, I would. No more oul Complan to get, and no more oul porridge to get, and no more...

Mag: (*Interrupting, holding her tea out*) No sugar in this, Maureen, you forgot, go and get me some.

Maureen's oxymoronic reply heightens the comedy in this scene, a darkly comical scene which establishes the grotesque bitterness of their relationship.

The last scene abounds in terrible pathos and hilarity, the one providing a bizarre, absurd context for the other. The previous scene, eerily set by Mag, motionless in her chair which rocks of its own volition, and Maureen idling about holding the poker, continues with Maureen's hallucinatory delusion of having seen Pato off at the train station with the promise of shortly joining him in America and ends with the Grand Guignol image of Mag toppling forward from her chair: '*A red chunk of skull hangs from a string of skin at the side of her head*' (McDonagh, 51). In the next scene Maureen brings in a suitcase and we assume she is preparing to go to America until Ray, that benighted messenger, arrives and disabuses her with, 'What station? Be taxicab Pato left' (McDonagh, 56). Thence the comedy, already set earlier by Ray's comparing the relative merits of Kimberley biscuits, Jaffa Cakes and Wagon Wheels, percolates alongside disaster. Ray, after telling Maureen that Pato was sad not to have seen her again, announces that Pato has become engaged to a girl in America. Maureen '*is dumbstruck*', descending further into madness as Ray chatters on breezily about Pato's fiancée's brown eyes, the priorities of European Championships football over weddings and the problems of matrimonial name changing:

> It won't be much of a change for her anyways, from Hooley to Dooley. Only one letter. The 'h'. That'll be a good thing. (*Pause*) Unless it's Healey that she is. I can't remember. (*Pause*) If it's Healey, it'll be three letters. The 'h', the 'e' and the 'a'. (57)

Maureen, stunned and confused, can only intone, 'Dolores Hooley'. The juxtaposition of the trivial and the tragic heighten them both and also suggest a Pirandellian concept of humour as a conflation of the ridiculous (Ray's inane chatter) and the sad (Maureen).

This intermesh of the trivial and the tragic – and sinister – is repeated when Maureen, enraged by Ray's scoffing at 'loons', advances on him with the poker and is distracted by his dispro-portionate, childish tantrum at finding a swingball confiscated by Maureen years ago. *'Maureen lets the poker fall to the floor with a clatter'* (McDonagh, 58), paving the way for another round of gallows humour with Ray's advice not to bang the poker against anything hard and Maureen promising that she won't. Finally, the comic dimension exits with Ray, leaving Maureen sitting in Mag's rocking chair, in Gothic nemesis, 'the exact fecking image' of her mother (McDonagh, 60). The play's inextricable admixture of the hilarious, the sad and the terrible haunts us with the caution that, 'What is funny had better not be laughed at'.[8]

In the *Beauty Queen* McDonagh ingeniously upholds and inverts basic components of the Irish dramatic canon and generic melo-drama generally. He retains the comic ingredient, mainly using licentious and macabre facets of humour, highlighting 'the tragic side of gaiety', dispersed throughout the dramatis personae rather than concentrated in a clown figure. This structure parallels the locus of evil as a presence inflecting sad victim-villains rather than as a singular, unmitigated personification of evil. Having said that, Ray with his addiction to Australian soaps and 'clobbering coppers' and debating the status of Kimberley biscuits versus Wagon Wheels could well be a modern-day clown figure.

In the wake of melodramatic precedent, the *Beauty Queen* articu-lates aspects of cultural transition in the Ireland of the 1990s. Notably, there is the demythologizing, indeed deconstruction, of the ideal family unit enshrined by much traditional melodrama and promulgated in a rustic utopia by Eamon de Valera. Not that earlier families were perfect, but miscreants (apart from the villain) almost always saw the error of their ways, and redemption and forgiveness, reconciliation of a sort or at least guilty regret, usually followed. This paradigm has been eroded over time, but in the

---

[8] Walter Kerr, *Tragedy and Comedy* (New York: Simon and Schuster, 1967), p.15.

Beauty Queen it is positively shattered in the morbidly dysfunctional relationship between Mag and Maureen, wherein mother-child bonding has twisted into venomous bondage. Here also, in keeping with the tenor of the play, can be assumed a double edge, on the one side dissecting familial tensions, which were always there but not often (before the advent of psychodynamic therapy) admitted; on the other side possibly relating to the wider context of contemporary family breakdown. Either way, de Valera's fantasy of 'cosy homesteads' and 'comely maidens' is harshly, and hilariously, demolished. Still in the realm of family matters lurks the quandary of the place of the old within the disintegration of the extended family, the burden on the carer, the problems of responsibility in a shifting value system. Emigration is lightly touched on, possibly because, with the recent expanding Irish economy, emigration is no longer the economic exigency it once was but still retains a vestigial place; perhaps because of the tentacles of history; perhaps because it offers escape from rural boredom, be it as insubstantial as Ray's fascination with drugs in Manchester and Australian soaps or as substantial as Pato's sense of 'psychic displacement', [9] not wanting be either here or there – the plight of many an emigrant, Irish or not. A factor that seems particularly to mark this play as belonging to the Ireland of the Nineties (or the Eighties) is the crude language and blatant sexuality, taboo areas in the Sixties and not really visible in the Seventies either. This seems to be contingent on a number factors: the major social revolution of the Sixties, the confluence of different cultures due to increased travel, the weakening hold of the Catholic Church, to name three. In the *Beauty Queen* McDonagh has demythologized the West of Ireland, assuredly, and echoes of the Irish dramatic canon reverberate throughout the play, yet a much broader context is unmistakeable; as John Peter comments,

---

[9] Christopher Murray, *Twentieth-Century Irish Drama* (Manchester: Manchester University Press, 1997), pp.170-175.

McDonagh's drama is 'universal but could be set nowhere except in Ireland'.[10]

Sources

Bentley, Eric, *The Life of the Drama* (New York: Applause, 1991).

Brooks, Peter, *The Melodramatic Imagination*. (Yale: University Press, 1995).

Freud, Sigmund. Jokes and Their Relation to the Unconscious. (London: Hogarth, 1964).

Ilsemann, Hartmut, 'Radicalism in the Melodrama of the Early Nineteenth Century' in *Melodrama: The Cultural Emergence of a Genre*, eds Michael Hays and Anastasia Nikolopoulou (London: Macmillan: 1999), pp.191-207.

Kerr, Walter, *Tragedy and Comedy* (New York: Simon and Schuster., 1967).

McCormick, John, 'Origins of Melodrama' in *Prompts 6* (Irish Theatre Archives, Sept. 1983), pp.5-12.

McDonagh, Martin, *The Beauty Queen of Leenane* in *Plays: 1* (London: Methuen, 1999).

Mercier, Vivian, *The Irish Comic Tradition*. (London: Souvenir, 1991).

Murray, Christopher, *Twentieth-Century Irish Drama*. (Manchester: Manchester University Press, 1997).

Oliver, Roger W., *Dreams of Passion: The Theatre of Luigi Pirandello*. (New York: New York University, 1979).

Pine, Richard, 'After Boucicault: Melodrama and the Modern Irish Stage' in *Prompts* (Irish Theatre Archives, Sept. 1983), pp.39-51.

Spencer, Charles, review of *The Beauty Queen of Leenane* in *The Daily Telegraph*, 8 March, 1996.

Rahill, Frank, *The World of Melodrama*. (Pennsylvania: State University Press, 1967).

Vandevelde, Karen, 'The Gothic Soap of Martin McDonagh' in *Theatre Stuff*, ed. by Eamonn Jordan (Dublin: Carysfort Press, 2000), pp.292-302.

---

[10] John Peter in Karen Vandevelde's 'The Gothic Soap of Martin McDonagh' in *Theatre Stuff*, ed. Eamonn Jordan (Dublin: Carysfort Press, 2000), pp.292-302, (p.299).

13 | Hamlet Versus The Rubber Chicken: The Learning Trajectory for a Theatre Practitioner

Declan Drohan

Actor: Personal learning from my own actor training

To the Greeks, comedy was current, always happening in the present tense, profoundly subversive, undermining of authority. Contemporary audiences have, however, a curious relationship with the form. On one hand, there is a voracious appetite for each *American Pie* or Adam Sandler outing, in a tradition leading right back to Aristophanes, finest proponent of the double entendre and the penis joke. On the other hand there is the unspoken assumption that great art is just *not funny,* and must edify us by earnestness and seriousness of purpose. In debunking and undermining cultural 'sacred cows', it also diminishes itself as a form. Humour is seen as disposable and of little cultural value.

Like most earnest, pretentious young men in actor training in the 1980s, I shared the prejudice without even being aware of it. Early experiences in the Gaiety School of Acting saw me mistake funny voices, odd walks and 'foreignness' for genuine contact with the audience. There was, within many of us, a deep-seated, culturally unchallenged belief that if we were to express more than a passing 'technical' interest in comic acting, we were somehow dishonouring Thespis' mighty lineage, abandoning Hamlet for the shallow possibilities of the rubber chicken.

I remember endlessly rehearsing a two-character exchange from O'Casey's *Silver Tassie* under the guidance of Pat Laffan, in which the protagonists are reticent to answer the phone in someone else's house. Probably exhausted by my small, self-conscious repertoire of comic devices, Pat kept urging me, with a curious crackle of irritability and enthusiasm, to speak in higher and higher registers, assuring me that this strategy would yield dividends. It certainly shocked me out of my habitual responses. In improvisation, I had been painfully earnest and pathologically crowd-pleasing, which, of course, pleased no-one by signalling neediness to an audience.

I recall one breakthrough in this area of work, an improvisation in which I played John Gielgud giving a fencing lesson to a young protégé. This sketch started from all the wrong premises, i.e., me doing something safe, an accent I already knew I could do well, seeking to impress Joe Dowling, who was running the session. But the manic physicality pushed me into unfamiliar territory, encouraged a heightened sense of real listening and real response to my partner. The bizarreness of the situation was inspiring, as it began to acknowledge its own artificiality. Eventually the fencing premise was discarded and we both began to converse in tremulous legato, as the Gielgud 'trumpet muted in silk' conceit dissolved into a series of exotic birdcalls. It was a moment of soaring liberation, and as I came down later, I wondered how I got there and if I could go there again. There was an interesting tension between the anarchy of the laughter we elicited and the control we had assumed in generating the piece.

This is the crux of the matter. In life, comedy is anarchic, spontaneous. It arises from context and specific circumstances. It is by nature hard to replicate. Actors deal continually with the difficulty of replicating rehearsal discoveries in performance. With the crude imprimatur of trying to make people laugh, the difficulties multiply considerably. It's often said that playing generality is the great enemy of precision in performance. This is even more the case in comic performance. This kind of communication needs absolute clarity; control is all. The actor must have a very defined grasp of the playing context. One can be clumsy, erratic and miss notes on the trajectory to a tragic climax. Not so in comedy.

In tragedy, if one can frame oneself within the 'given circumstances' of character, plot, personal history, etc., the story will unfold. Regardless of the subtlety or detail of the experience, there is some satisfaction for the audience in merely being witnesses to this unfolding. If you signal to the audience in advance that this material is intended to be funny, then you create another hurdle for the actors. They may strain, they may force the carefully established pace from the rehearsal period. The audience may not laugh. They may possibly become uncomfortable, restless, even irritable. While individuals in the audience may be amused to some extent by elements of what's being witnessed, the actor may feel there is a sort of 'moral majority' response in operation, pushing towards a collective agreement about what is funny. 'A thing is either funny or not' is the impatient subtext the actor projects onto his audience. There is no leeway for partial success. This is fine in cinema where the actors are absent. In live performance, however, the non-response of the audience can further distort the pace and shape of the performances. They don't laugh, you begin to panic, you try too hard. You force the pace, throwing away all of the detail established in rehearsal. You don't trust yourself, your lines, your colleagues, the director, gravity. You are supposed to be in control, not merely of your own pre-planned pattern of movement and utterance, but also of their experience as an audience.

So how do you avoid the above circumstance? Firstly, holding back in rehearsal to save 'something special for the opening' is completely out. Praying for some miracle of alchemy to occur in the presence of the audience transmuting lead into gold is naïve and superstitious. *More* energy is required than in other kinds of rehearsal, or, more precisely, a higher degree of risk taking. And as the structure emerges through engagement with the living process of rehearsal, trust it, believe in it, inhabit it and let it inhabit you. Never apologize in front of an audience, or even in a rehearsal room. While their responses are varied, there is a general contract among audience members that he who opens the oven door is responsible for ruining the soufflé, bursting the bubble, that is, drawing the audience's attention to the artificiality of the encounter, the self-consciousness of being perceived.

It is impossible and of absolutely no value to 'walk through' a comic play in rehearsal. Each run-through, with or without observers, must attempt to lock into the newly discovered dynamic,

observing its tensions and elasticity. Even prior to previews and
first-night audiences, there exists a complex web of pre-expressive
difficulties in comic acting.

The primary difficulty lies in mediating the relationship with the
audience: managing transitions, switching from talking to other
characters to direct address to the onlookers, acknowledging them
in asides, glances, acknowledging complicity. As actor/director
Simon Callow observes:

> The difficulty for the actor is how to cast the audience. Who are
> they? They are all absolutely different people with different
> experiences of life. How does one simultaneously talk to them all?
> How does one find an intimate relationship with them? The simple
> answer is that in an aside, a character is addressing his peers.

There is an inherent difficulty of expectation in this under-
taking: it's not just about how clever the writing is. Will they
actually laugh? You can't just 'trust the words' and tell the story.
You need immediate, not delayed feedback. In tragedy, you have
time to draw them in. In comedy, you must establish the terms of
this complex relationship *immediately* – or perish.

Teacher: What I've Learned About Playing/Directing Comedy through my Teaching Work

In the Conservatory of Music and Drama, D.I.T. Rathmines, I was
asked to teach a theoretical/practical block on Restoration theatre.
Through this work, over three or four years, I learned about *scale* –
that being conversational, naturalistic is too understated and does
not generate enough energy for this genre of performance.
Language *is* action in these plays. On the other hand, we must also
be careful to avoid playing caricatures rather than individuals, as
audiences disengage immediately if there is no core to the figures
before them.

Mr Callow has interesting things to say about sentence structure
and the imperative for the actor to think through to the end of a
sentence, in plays of this genre, regardless of the number of inter-
vening, contesting clauses. Every inflection must be intentional,
every word weighed and measured, every character decision clear
and visible. The extent to which the audience are complicit in

whatever deception is being perpetrated at this point in the action must also be clearly established. As in Shakespeare, asides are very often where subtext and self-examination take place. Collusion is established in these instances.

No matter how preposterous, inflated, or exaggerated characters appear initially, they must also establish, in some sense, their fundamental honesty. This is, I am aware, a problematic word to use in the context of artifice in this age of post-modernism, New Historicism, simultaneous and virtual reality, etc. What I mean is that the actor must install, sustain and convey the character's internal life in a way that is readily communicable to an audience. This core must be maintained throughout the trajectory of the play. A collection of ticks, routines, and 'turns' will not always suffice. Oftentimes, the performer must work hard to earn laughter. It is odd that some kinds of pretence seem more 'honest' than others.

There is also a tension between people's perceptions of 'natural' comic ability versus a detailed work process. The assumption that comic timing/ability is innate creates a barrier for some young actors. People pass on all kinds of esoteric, handed-down wisdoms in discussing comic timing and ability, making no more sense than the Alan Alda director figure in Woody Allen's *Crimes and Misdemeanors*: 'If it bends it's funny; if it breaks it's not'. Fetishizing 'talent' over meticulous work process is a minefield. A sense of comic timing is useful, but most comic characters, quite rightly, should have no sense that they're funny. Musicality is useful – building, establishing and breaking rhythms. Just when audiences feel they can predict character action, it must change somehow.

Working on canonical texts like Congreve's *The Way of the World* and Sheridan's *School for Scandal* also exposes the intellectually lazy student. The most common error lies in mistaking fops and dandies for gay characters. Nothing could be further from the truth – they are rapacious, predatory dandies, gleefully keeping the audience abreast of the double crosses and intrigues which fuel the unfolding plots. Typically, these plays are about intrigue, sexual competitiveness, duplicity, fortune-hunting, and confused identity. 'True love' is often portrayed as the province of the dim or intellectually limited. Yes, we have the convention observed of true love found, lost, and 'happy ever after' – but it's often delivered with a wink or in parentheses. There are much more cynical, subversive forces at work here.

Chekhov is particularly interesting from the point of view of the comic/tragic tension possible at the heart of highly evolved writing and performance. If acting is about the accumulation of detail, and about the culmination of choices/decisions throughout the rehearsal process, then in the case of Chekhov, we are faced with a blizzard of possibility. Because of the opacity/ indeterminacy of the dialogue and the inertia and inaction of the characters, our selection of approach or initial performative response virtually 're-writes' the play in each performance instance. Discussion of the play under consideration can frame the approach. Directorial concept can set an agenda. But only in the rehearsal space can decisive and narrative defining spadework be done on the material. Chekhov's is a comedy of recognition. We discern the essential selfishness of the characters, we acknowledge that the self-absorption of the characters creates behavioural comedy.

The lessons of Chekhov's observational or character-based comedy have long since been absorbed into the mainstream. Situation comedy is a crude derivative of these discoveries, portraying characters often unaware of their own shortcomings, their effect on others. Adherence to characterization, rather than the short term need to 'get laughs', and to our shared experience of human frailty achieves resonance in contact/exchange with other characters. It is a humour of sympathy, empathy, recognition and identification.

The problem in staging 'canonical' plays is the proliferation of preconceptions or accepted articles of faith which cloud our paths of approach. Like parasitic creeping fungi, they must be scraped away to reveal the specific details of the organism beneath.

Jonathan Miller's analogy of treating an overly familiar speech from a play as fossil fragment which may, through close analysis, reveal the outline of the larger creature still unearthed, is also useful. I contribute a combined lecture/workshop component to the M.A. in Drama in St. Patrick's College, Drumcondra, on approaches to playing Chekhov, which has demonstrated over time that a comic reading of these texts is as viable as the elegiac tremor and sob of a stereotypical Stanislavski interpretation. We recognize the self-absorption and selfishness of the characters and wince or giggle at the monstrous impasses of neediness or self-pity which propel the plays.

Director: *Tartuffe* Discoveries

My approach to the staging of *Tartuffe* in Sligo in Spring 2003 was predetermined by things I learned teaching Restoration comedy under workshop conditions – ignoring the obvious, external dressings of the piece, period, and costume, and instead, trying to locate the play within the interplay of character and patterns of movement, actual and implied, physical, psychological and social, within the piece.

My decision to write a new version/translation was entirely utilitarian at first – I didn't want to pay royalties. But as work progressed I became aware of a number of elements within the framework of the piece that for me were essential:

1. Orgone's brother is a wholly redundant character, serving only as a sounding board for Orgone, and an ally for some of the house's inhabitants. Cutting him makes the plight of the house's inhabitants even more stark – they have no champion, no external ally. Some of his content, important in terms of establishing elements of plot, went to Damis (Dennis, in my version).

2. From Molière's text, we have no sense of Tartuffe's power to preach or hypnotize. Indeed, he is so grotesque that his attractiveness to women is rendered entirely inexplicable. This was perhaps one of Molière's own concessions to the French Catholic Church in the light of their initial objections to the play. I introduced extracts from 'Song of Solomon' as his preaching text, to open and close the play and serve as a bridge between scenes. If we had proceeded along the route of exploring and examining Tartuffe's (and consequently, Molière's) attitude to women, a different production would have ensued.

3. I was never happy with the conventional understanding of the central Tartuffe/Elmira relationship. I always felt that this highly moral creature would never behave this way toward Tartuffe if she wasn't a little in love with him. A by-product of her husband's new religious zeal is that he ignores her. She is insecure,

filling Orgone's deceased first wife's shoes, parenting his grown-up children, and on the receiving end of her mother-in-law's scorn. She turns to this hypnotic creature who flatters and openly desires her.

4. Characters must speak in sentences *not* paragraphs. Extant versions of the play seem inflated, verbose. From the very beginning, I was clear that my *Tartuffe* would not exceed one hour and fifteen minutes in playing time.

5. The ending of the play as written is unsatisfactory and smacks of compromise and conservatism. All's well that ends well? There are strong resonances in the Irish context with the discovery of Catholic Church sex and state-concealed financial scandals of recent years. Our Tartuffe relocates to the next parish and starts all over again. Elmira's 'A happy ending …' is wistful and bittersweet.

6. Following on from the foregoing, this Tartuffe was set in a rural Irish, non-specific late 1940s, early 1950s 'golden age of innocence', before clerical abuse, government scandals, tribunals, etc. We quite pointedly cast an actor who was every inch the bony, bespectacled, ascetic Irish Catholic Priest of this period. The subplot about missing government documents and close relationships between wealthy property owners and the state was also a very contemporary one. Without overloading Tartuffe with these elements and allowing it to sink under the weight of 'relevance', it is possible to make these connections playfully without distorting the central premise of the work.

Calling Orgone 'Doctor (Terence) O'Reilly in this version is a deliberate link to a putative Tony O'Reilly figure. This is an elliptical reference to the proliferation of New Age and alternative mind, body and spiritual practices in contemporary Ireland, and the dissatisfaction with conventional belief systems. The utter stupidity of the lovers Val and Marianne is more extreme in this version, indicating that our serious attention should lie elsewhere.

7. Rather than being grotesque, Tartuffe must seem plausible as a guru, lover and leader. If we remove the surface ugliness, then there is more tension in the piece. It adds depth if, rather than being a complete charlatan, Tartuffe believes every word he says, believes he has the powers attributed to him.

8. Mrs. Parnell (Mme. Pernelle) is emblematic of an older generation of Irish person who, in the face of overwhelming evidence, refuses to accept incontestable facts re clerical abuse or questionable financial practices of leading political parties.

Rehearsal Process: Between Thought and Expression

Unlike my student groups in D.I.T., the pool of possible actors from the newly founded Drama Society at I.T. Sligo had no shared history of prior theatre experiences – some had professional training, some amateur experiences, and some had no previous exposure to any kind of drama practice. An early in-house, chorus-focussed *Agamemnon* prepared the group to some extent for the kind of rigour and detail I would expect of them. The first step with *Tartuffe* was to create a culture of work which established ensemble values and clarified that no role was more important than any other, and that characters would never leave the playing space, 'witnessing' the scenes they were not directly involved in.

Initial workshopping was intensely energized, establishing behavioural traits, and the specific physicality of each proposed character. I found that no matter how often I reminded the actors to sustain high levels of energy, in the style of silent-movie actors, they consistently underestimated what was required. There was for many of the performers an assumption that somehow, miraculously, this level of engagement was appropriate to performance but not rehearsal. I specifically built in-between-scene moments where characters frenetically gossiped and mingled to ensure that no-one disengaged or lost focus. I also required the actors to double as servants, churchgoers and eavesdroppers in an effort to work inventively within the spare design concept of the stage setting, providing simultaneous description and exposition. I did miss the physical fluidity of trained actors who would have a culture of movement and dance training underpinning their work, however subconsciously. However, pace and clarity of exposition somewhat compensated for these shortfalls.

The most frequent notes given in early run-throughs were, 'I can't hear you!' and ' Faster, more energy!' No matter how crude the characterizations or clumsy the staging initially, I was determined that the performers should be clear what the minimum level of engagement should be. Also, in such a dense text, with so much extraneous detail cut away, no line could be thrown away from the perspective of characterization and narrative clarity. It was important for this group of actors to trust the visual telling of the tale – that contained within each freeze frame constructed by us in initial workshops to encapsulate each scenic unit, much character detail was already clear. Subsequent dialogue could confirm or challenge initial responses. Simply, we needed to trust the audience to 'read' the onstage relationships, rather than crudely signal our opinion or attitude in our first moments of audience contact.

It is difficult, too, for inexperienced and experienced actors alike to avoid playing out or 'implying', in early scenes, their full knowledge of the character and the outcome of the story yet to unfold. This is particularly true in comedy of this kind, with a strong element of melodrama, where the rollercoaster movement of incident, disclosure, and confrontation is so extreme. Jean Genet's belief that each scene should be played as if it is a free-standing, self-contained unit was a useful guide at this point in the work. And yet for the actors, the greatest complexity came from timing the delivery of the blatant double entendres that pepper the text, and discovering the nature of their relationship with the audience:

> 'My prayers are poor things, yet, all my ejaculations have been on your behalf.'
> 'Maybe if you suck on something…a barley sugar perhaps?'

More problematic still were lines in which contemporary resonance vied with the narrative thrust of the play – for example, the sequence in which Tartuffe feigns concern for Dennis as his father threatens him physically. We established that Tartuffe should play the peacemaker, delivering most of the dialogue to the two other figures on stage, while saving the italicized portion for direct audience address:

> In the name of God be still! I would suffer any blow to shield this boy from your wrath! *The family is sacred to me!*'

In a contemporary Irish setting, to see a figure dressed in clerical garb speaking these words when his actions are so at odds with the spoken sentiment often provoked the harsh uneasy laughter of identification – how is it that we are not so quick to spot hypocrisy and lies when we see them in actuality?

Opening the play in an unfamiliar, traditional, proscenium-arch venue in Tubbercurry was exactly the white-knuckle adrenaline rush the actors needed to galvanize them into a coherent working unit. One week in our own Black Box space at the Institute of Technology, Sligo, saw the play move into a period of consolidation, detail and precision. Our final performances at D.I.T. Rathmines, Dublin, and the Hawkswell Theatre Sligo were rich and nuanced in their playful tension between narrative line, contemporary resonances, and the slow wink of the assured performer in the telling of the tale.

And the learning curve for me, on this extended, largely unplanned journey from actor, through teacher, to director over the past fifteen years? All communication in theatre operates on a spider web of tensions and oppositions. Rather than being problematic, this leads us into a forest of paradox and possibility, which we must embrace. We rehearse the performance but the performance must seem spontaneous. The words we speak are (in most cases) pre-written, yet we must spend weeks discovering, unearthing them. We may spend years studying 'technique(s)' of one kind or another, yet in performance we must abandon technique so that our skill doesn't appear self-regarding, nor does it unbalance the ensemble. We rehearse and perform works which are sometimes culturally, politically and intellectually dense and complex with the aim of rendering them with simplicity and clarity. Instinct informs experience. Experience informs instinct. There is the danger that we fall into the trap of formulae, tricks and comfort zones throughout a career.

Ideally, we should treat each rehearsal period, each performance encounter as an entirely distinct entity from the ones before. The greatest compliment you could possibly be paid, looking back over a body of work, would be that you never developed a recognizable style. And yet even the most eclectic performers and directors develop over time a signature as identifiable as a fingerprint. This is particularly true of performers who are drawn to comic material. They are cast for this readily familiar – therefore accessible – style, this rapport. To embody an everyman figure perhaps, one must play close to oneself, stripping away layers of characterization rather than adding to them, simplifying rather than complicating. And that's the journey. To learn to be yourself, not a reflection of your teachers, actors and directors you've admired, gurus or heroes. The journey is circular and leads you right back to yourself.

Sources

Callow, Simon, *Acting in Restoration Comedy* (New York: Applause Theatre Books, 1991).

Guthrie, Tyrone, *A Life in The Theatre* (New York: Limelight Editions, 1985).

Guthrie, Tyrone, *In Various Directions* (London The Hollen Street Press; 1965).

Hall, Peter, *Peter Hall's Diaries*, ed. John Goodwin (London: Hamish Hamilton Ltd; 1983).

Harwood, Ronald, *All the World's a Stage* (London: Secker & Warburg; 1984).

Leggatt, Alexander. *English Stage Comedy 1490-1990, Five Centuries of a Genre* (London and New York: Routledge; 1998).

Miller, Jonathan, *Subsequent Performances* (London: Faber & Faber; 1986).

Saivetz, Deborah, *An Event in Space: JoAnne Akalataitis in Rehearsal* (New Hampshire: Smith and Kraus Inc, 2000).

14 | Playing the Body: Marina Carr's Comedy of (Bad) Manners

Melissa Sihra

Marina Carr's second play, *Low In The Dark*, was first produced by the Crooked Sixpence Theatre Company at the Project Arts Centre, Dublin, in 1989. In this 'homage to Beckett', Carr's employment of metatheatrical strategies such as role-play and cross-dressing comically subverts conventional representations of gender and the body, emphasizing through play the performativity of everyday social codes and practices. Each one of Carr's early (unpublished) plays *The Deer's Surrender* (Andrew's Lane Theatre, 1990), *This Love Thing* (Tinderbox / Pigsback Theatre Company, Project Arts Centre, 1991) and *Ullaloo* (Peacock Theatre, 1991) explores the possibilities of non-realism through elements of absurdist theatre. In the program note of *Ullaloo* playwright Tom Mac Intyre, who is also known for the radical physicality of his plays, refers to the reception of the earlier *Low In The Dark*.

> Watching the play, watching the audiences, it was fascinating to feel in the spectators the excitement of being participants in something *now*, being in on a piece which stretched them thematically and stylistically.[1]

Irish drama can traditionally be characterized by its preoccupation with predominantly nationalist, masculinist, colonial and post-colonial explorations of identity, in which the 'literary' is privileged

---

[1] Tom Mac Intyre, Program Note for *Ullaloo,* Peacock Theatre, March 1991.

over an awareness of physicality, performance and female subjectivity.

With its emphasis on issues of gender and sexuality, *Low In The
Dark* was a pioneering work in 1989 and is one of the first Irish
plays to consider physicality and the body as central to both the
form and content. Similarly, the politics of gender representation,
sexuality and corporeality are finally emerging with force and consistency in the recent critical discourse concerning Irish theatre,
past and present.

Low In The Dark marked, along with Mac Intyre's work, a
turning point in Irish theatrical representation, where a new
physical form of theatre was emerging and where artistic col-
laboration and the process of devising was integral. In her account
of the rehearsal process actor Sarahjane Scaife recalls:

> Marina would write at night and come in the next day with a new
> scene. We would play the scene and then play with it. Afterwards
> we would talk about what worked and what didn't. Marina would
> then revise what she felt was necessary.[2]

Ireland in the 1980s was relatively univocal in terms of the arts in
general and theatre in particular, and there was little cross-
disciplinary work. A play was strictly word-based and the idea of
actors being trained in the use of their bodies was just starting.
Mac Intyre comments on the theatricality and experimental spirit
of *Low In The Dark:*

> What makes this playwright's work especially exciting is the manner
> in which she blends boldness with an adventurous approach to
> form. A large part of the fun in her two recent plays – *Low In The
> Dark* and *This Love Thing* – had to do with her healthy willingness
> to discard traditional forms.[3]

Crooked Sixpence is the only company to date to stage this
work professionally in Ireland and another production is long
overdue. The show was directed by Philip Hardy with Brid Mhic

---

2 Sarahjane Scaife, 'Mutual Beginnings: Marina Carr's *Low in the Dark*', in *The
   Theatre of Marina Carr: before rules was made"*, Cathy Leeney and Anna
   McMullan, eds (Dublin: Carysfort Press, 2003), p.6.
3 Tom Mac Intyre, Program Note for *Ullaloo,* Peacock Theatre, March 1991.

Fhearai playing the role of Curtains, Joan Brosnan Walshe playing
Bender, Sarahjane Scaife playing Binder and Peter Holmes and
Dermod Moore playing Baxter and Bone respectively. With *Low in
the Dark* emerged a voice that openly addressed, within a non-
realistic frame, issues such as childbirth, sexuality, mother-and-
daughter relationships and the sexist ideology, language and ex-
clusionist patriarchal politics of the Catholic Church. Scaife
observes:

> I don't think I was conscious of it at the time, but retrospectively,
> the facts of Marina's sex and youth removed her from the tra-
> ditional male hierarchy that had been predominant in theatre in
> Ireland. Theatre was run by men for the most part. Plays were
> directed by men and written by men.[4]

The play is a hilarious romp with gender in which issues of
identity, sexuality and the body are shown to be socially determined, within a playful yet explicitly feminist framework.
'Gender' occurs when culture is mapped onto the biological body,
and in *Low In The Dark* the body is the central site in which social
codes and meanings are inscribed. Throughout the drama Carr
humorously deconstructs fixed notions of gender identity and
plays with the socially cultivated signifiers of masculinity, femininity and heterosexuality. In 1991 Mac Intyre acutely identified the
playwright's nascent preoccupation: '[Carr] applies herself to her
persistent theme – A man, a woman; a woman, a man.' Each one
of Carr's early plays contemplates the fraught yet mutually
dependent relationship between men and women and the world
which they cohabit, and while absurdist in style and tone, vividly
sets the stage for the emotional landscapes of her later tragedies.

As indicated in the *dramatis personae* of *Low In The Dark,* we are
presented initially with two 'males' called Baxter and Bone and
three 'females' called Bender, Binder and Curtains who are representative of abstract types rather than 'recognizable' individuals.
The *mise en scène* is divided simply in two, with stage left denoting a:
'*Bizarre bathroom; bath, toilet and shower, a brush with hat and tails on it,*
[and stage right,] *The men's space; tyres, unfinished walls and blocks*

---

4 Scaife, p.6.

strewn about.[5] Carr's juxtaposition of the 'men's space' with the 'bizarre bathroom' (denoting the 'female' space), ironically sets-up the playing space for the forthcoming gender destabilizations. Through techniques of defamiliarization, inversion and subversive humour, Carr effectively highlights the absurdity and confinement of social and ideological structures through parody, non-linear plot and symbolic characterization. The rapid scene-changes, quick-fire dialogue and continual layers of overlapping role-play in *Low In The Dark* present a world in which 'normativity' is rendered increasingly uncertain, excessive and maniacal. Martin Esslin, the critic who coined the term Absurdism in 1961, defines it thus:

> The Theatre of the Absurd strives to express its sense of the senselessness of the human condition and the inadequacy of the rational approach by the open abandonment of rational devices and discursive thought.[6]

In Carr's play we can see the ways in which the ostensible 'non-sensicality' and hyperbole of the form, as previously employed by Samuel Beckett, becomes an effective and radical means by which to comment on the absurdism of the everyday. Mac Intyre writes:

> *Low In The Dark*, particularly, realised a zany equilibrium form, a melange which included slapstick, cartoon, gender-bending, song, dance, storytelling, lyric interlude and ebullient dialogue.[7]

With the exception of Curtains, each character engages in compulsive gender impersonation and mimicry throughout the drama, playing out states of cacophonic and, at times, manic topsy-turvy senselessness. The intriguingly named Curtains is the only character in the play whose initial gender assignation remains seemingly 'female' throughout the drama.

---

[5] Marina Carr, *Marina Carr Plays: One,* (London: Faber & Faber, 1999), p.5. All future references to the text of *Low in the Dark* will be noted by the page number(s) from this edition in parenthesis.

[6] Martin Esslin, 'The Theatre of the Absurd', in William, B Worthen, *The Harcourt Brace Anthology of Drama,* Third Edition, (Boston: Thomson and Heimle, 2000), pp.876-7.

[7] Tom Mac Intyre, Program Note of *Ullaloo.*

Elusive and enigmatic, the figure of Curtains is the central storyteller in the drama. Carr describes this figure as being:

> any age, as she is covered from head to toe in heavy, brocaded curtains and rail. Not an inch of her face or body is seen throughout the play. (5)

Curtains's ornate brocaded material conceals or 'curtains' her throughout. Opening and closing the action with her ongoing narrative, Curtains' costume of curtains become a playful referent to traditional proscenium staging, suggestively embodying the dynamics of theatrical performance. Like Polonius masquerading behind the cloth in *Hamlet,* Curtains is a 'play within a play', a screen-scene richly metatheatrical. Inviting 'opening' and fuelling suspense, Curtains' curtained body is seductively removed from the politicized economy of visibility, challenging traditional modes of female corporeal representation, or what Laura Mulvey refers to as the quality of 'to-be-looked-at-ness'.[8] Scaife recalls Brid Mhic Fhearrai's performance of Curtains:

> Brid had real difficulty in finding a path to play the part as she could not use her physicality in the normal way, being shrouded in curtains! However, through this restriction she found a new freedom for her voice, which was probably the idea.'[9]

The incessant role-playing and cross-dressing in *Low In The Dark* makes it increasingly difficult for the spectator to ascertain who is who throughout the course of the action. In an interview Carr comments: 'Who is male and who is female in *Low In The Dark?* I don't know, they are all mixed, one or the other.'[10] In Scene Three of Act One the two 'males', Bone and Baxter, perform the roles of a stereotypical heterosexual couple:

> **Bone:** Make it up. Come on.
> **Baxter:** (*woman's voice*) Do you like my lipstick?

---

[8] Laura Mulvey, 'Visual Pleasure and Narrative Cinema' in *The Routledge Reader in Gender and Performance*, eds Liz Goodman and Jane Gay, (London & New York: Routledge, 1998), p.272.

[9] Scaife, p.15.

[10] Marina Carr, Interview with Melissa Sihra (unpublished), Trinity College, Dublin, February 25, 1999.

Bone: Yes, I do.
Baxter: And my sock?
Bone: Yes.
Baxter: I want a baby.
Bone: So do I.
Baxter: Will you buy me a present?
Bone: You want to trap me.
Baxter: I need you Bone.
Bone: You don't.
Baxter: Alright, I don't.
Bone: No! You do.
Baxter: I do.
Bone: You don't.
Baxter: I don't.
Bone: You do!
Baxter: I don't!
Bone: You do!
Baxter: No, you need me! (41-2)

Theatre is an ideal forum within which to re-imagine conservative notions of corporeality, sexuality and gendered identity due to its performative nature. In *Low In the Dark* gendered identity is continually parodied, as cross-dressed characters inhabit, perform and crucially, *play* with the cultural signifiers of conventional gendered identity, offering a disruption of social normativity. The 'women', Bender and Binder, are allocated the uniforms and props of their gender – lipstick, handbags, tampons, The Pill, necklaces, high heels and scarves – while the men are given a Black and Decker D.I.Y. tool kit, bricks, hats and tails. When these articles are handled by the opposite sex, their cultural and semiotic values are radically altered and re-politicized. This is illustrated in Scene Three of Act Two, when Baxter and Bone perform stereotypes of hetero-normativity: Bone, who plays the husband, begins the action: 'Ready'. Baxter *does a little walk, then turns.* [...] *Woman's voice:* 'Hello, darling.' *They kiss.* How was your day?' Baxter replies: 'Fine, and yours? Painting your nails again?' Bone says: 'Yes, it's wearing off. Are you hungry?' (40)

Marjorie Garber notes that role-playing and cross-dressing are 'fundamentally related to other kinds of boundary-crossing'.[11] Such boundary-crossing in performance can reveal, subvert and contest the very real ideological boundary structures of dominant and marginal identities. Bone and Baxter engage in more role-play, displaying through defamiliarization the artificiality of prescribed gender roles and objects: *'Bone has his arm around Baxter as if they are a married couple. Baxter wears high heels, a woman's hat, a dress, and a necklace around his neck. He looks pregnant.'* (16) In *Low In The Dark*, naturalized gender behaviour is humorously identified when projected onto the politicized sites of the performing 'crossed' bodies, and simple, everyday activities such as knitting and building are re-contextualized to highlight their implicit ideology.

> **Baxter:** (*Woman's voice*) You're marvellous, darling, you really are.
> **Bone:** (*Pointing to the wall*) So you like it?... I think you should do your knitting.
> **Baxter:** I want to help with the wall!
> **Bone:** Knit darling, knit! (*Brief tableau of knitting and building*) (16)

The repetitive action of building and knitting points to the binding imprisonment of rigid genderization. In Scene Three, Baxter and Bone resume their role-play, as *'Bone enters, lays a brick, sits in a deck-chair and starts knitting. Baxter arrives with a necklace around his neck and nail polish in his hand'.* (38) The characters swap the gender-signifying objects back and forth:

> **Baxter:** (*Offering the nail polish again*) Look, will you do this or won't you?
> **Bone:** Always the necklace!
> **Baxter:** Always the knitting!
> *Baxter gives him the nail polish. Bone sits down, takes off a shoe and begins to paint his toenails in a female pose.* (39)

In the same way that Beckett's theatre is concerned with the dehumanizing effects of repetition, in plays such as *Act Without Words II*, *Krapp's Last Tape*, or *Waiting for Godot*, Binder poignantly comments in Scene Five on the vicious circularity of everyday

---

[11] Marjorie Garber, 'Cross-Dressing, Gender and Representation', in *The Feminist Reader*, eds Catherine Belsey and Jane Moore (London: Macmillan Press, 1997), p.165.

social patterns and behaviour: 'I knit, he builds, he builds, he knocks it down and he builds again.'(53)

While they are role-playing, Bone and Baxter switch in and out of their assigned genders and gender performances at various points. In the stage directions Carr ironically notes that the '*real Baxter erupts out of the role-play*' switching from '*a deep man's voice*' back to '*a feminine voice*'. (17) This anti-realistic embodiment emphasizes the conscious performativity of the enactments and confounds the notion of the unified subject. In the same scene Baxter, the male 'wife', says, 'You're not earning enough! [...] I think you should get another job.' Bone replies, 'But I'd never see you!' Baxter, in his 'real voice' retorts, 'Exactly!' Bone takes offence: 'Watch it!', to which Baxter plays the 'niggling female again': 'Is there any point in us going on?' (18)

In highlighting the absurdity of extreme gender binaries, Michelene Wandor notes how cross-dressing in performance:

> can function as an expression of rebellion; a form of witty subversion in which one sex impersonates the other, and by so doing shows up some of the ridiculous constraints which define femininity and masculinity.[12]

Cross-dressing on stage reveals the artifice and social performativity of gender construction within the greater social context. Most notably, performance theorist Judith Butler observes the ways in which cross-dressing can interrogate and indeed shatter the 'illusion of coherence' or the sense of an essential or innate, 'natural-born' unity and stability in relation to conventional notions of masculine and feminine identities. In *Gender Trouble: Feminism and the Subversion of Identity,* she writes:

> The appearance of cross-dressed bodies playing with the visible ornaments of gender displaces the inner/outer boundary of the

---

[12] Michelene Wandor, 'Cross-dressing, Sexual Representation and the Sexual Division of Labour in the Theatre' in *The Routledge Reader in Gender and Performance,* p.172.

body and exposes the illusion of coherence and unified origin in constructions of gender.[13]

Act Two of *Low In The Dark* shows Baxter and Bone consumed with performing stereotypical tropes of femininity. Baxter sees that Bone is holding a woman's earring and a pink sock and asks, 'Can I, eh, can I try it on? […] How does she walk?' Bone replies, 'I haven't quite mastered it yet, but it's something like this.' The character '[d]oes a female walk' and 'Baxter copies him'. (22-3)

In the same scene Bone is 'back in the female role' and Baxter asserts, 'Red's your colour'. Bone repeats, 'Red's my colour'. Baxter then says, 'And sometimes rust', to which Bone blandly responds, 'And sometimes rust'. Highlighting the meaninglessness and interchangeability of the gender identities, Baxter then says, 'OK, it's my turn now. (*He takes the necklace, puts the lid on the polish and puts the necklace around his neck.*)' (41)

The relationship between clothing and the body is fundamental to cultural and ontological signification. Roland Barthes notes that without clothing the body cannot actually signify meaning and that clothing is our 'passage from sentience to meaning; it is we might say, the signified par excellence.'[14] If gender only exists in re-presentation, and clothing is, as Barthes argues, the main signifier of the representation, what is *beneath* the clothes? Can the body thus be regarded as a socially constructed entity? As Butler provocatively asserts: 'The imitations [of gendered identity] effectively displace the meaning of the original, they imitate the myth of originality itself'.[15] Carr's depiction of the curtained Curtains, a figure of all clothing and no body, complicates the notion of the body as a stable social text. We are presented with a clothed 'no-body' and can only construct the character's identity based upon the material evidence (or signification) of the costume.

---

[13] Judith Butler, *Gender Trouble; Feminism and the Subversion of Identity* (New York: Routledge, 1990), pp.132-4.

[14] Roland Barthes, *The Fashion System,* trans. Matthew Ward and Richard Howard (New York: 1983), p.258.

[15] Judith Butler, 'Gender Trouble' in *Feminist Theory and the Body; A Reader* eds J. Price, and M. Shildrick (Edinburgh: Edinburgh University Press, 1999), p.418.

Throughout the play there is an emphasis on physical bodily acts and functions such as copulation, birth, eating, drinking, death and defecation. In Scene Five of Act Two, the male Bone describes being born and giving birth:

> the groaning, the blood, the shit, the piss, and the first scream, there was the point of no return. A rough start to a rough journey I tell you. I wouldn't wish life on my worst enemy, I'll have an abortion. (80)

Baxter comments, 'We're all abortions, some later than others, that's all. But look on the good side. Life is short, soon we'll be dead.' The visceral quality of this exchange remains topical as, after two referenda in the 1990s, abortion remains an illegal act in Ireland. The dialogue of *Low In The Dark* is abundant with vivid images of the lower bodily stratum of carnivalesque grotesque realism which, according to Mikhail Bakhtin, are 'such leading themes as copulation, pregnancy, birth, eating, drinking and death'.[16] Bender, Binder's mother, is first seen in the bath in Act One, giving birth for the umpteenth time. Here mother and daughter enact the stereotype of a 'long-suffering' married couple:

> **Binder:** You've put on weight!
> **Bender:** That's the baby.
> **Binder:** You drink too much!
> **Bender:** I don't drink half enough! I deserve one after that ordeal. […] Put him in the shower and give him a doll!
> **Binder:** They're for girl-babies.
> **Bender:** Well then give him a train and give his mother a drink! (8-9)

Countless babies of different colour are born throughout *Low In The Dark*, and are then flung carelessly to and fro as their genders oscillate indiscriminately. The stage-directions indicate, '*Curtains throws a yellow baby at Bender, and throws a pink one at Binder. […] The yellow baby is swapped for the pink baby. All three of them are involved in the throwing and the catching*'. (52) In Scene Five of Act One:

> Binder goes to the shower, throws three babies on Bender and sits with two, both breast-feeding. Curtains gets up and goes over to

---

16   Mikhail Bakhtin, *Rabelais and his World,* trans. Helene Iswolsky, (Bloomington: Indiana University Press, 1984), p.355.

the shower. She grabs an armful of babies, and orchestrates the feeding of the babies. Soundtrack of babies gurgling and crying comes over. (51)

Scaife notes the theatricality of the staging:

There were dozens of babies made of wrapped, stuffed cotton, with different colour codes. In the bath, Bender was constantly dropping babies and feeding them, and demanding more. Bender and myself had fantastic John Paul Gaultier style boned costumes with cone shaped 'boobs'. The 'boobs' unzipped to reveal babies' faces on them. We were constantly unzipping them to feed the babies. (10)

In the carnivalesque atmosphere of praise and abuse ambivalence, the babies are thrown about the stage, beaten indiscriminately, then fawned upon. After throwing away one of the many babies, Binder states, 'He's a very ugly baby!' Bender then kisses the baby and gives it to Binder who continues, 'I think it's a she. (*Throws it in the shower*)'.(11) That the babies' genders may change at any given time, a notion ironically naturalized into the narrative, indicates the playful indeterminacy which runs throughout the drama. In the same scene, Binder, who is breast-feeding Bender's baby, declares, 'It's a she!' to which Binder replies, 'What'll we call him?'(9)

Rabelaisian irreverence permeates *Low in the Dark* when the babies are given humorously inappropriate or incongruous names. In Scene Five of Act One, Bender says:

I know my children! This is the Doctor! Here on my right breast is the Black Sheep! (*Points to the yellow one.*) On my left, the President! Now, where's the Pope?

The carnivalesque impulse of laughter as a subversive mode of recalcitrance to dominant authority runs riot throughout the narrative of *Low in the Dark*. Bender says of her latest baby, 'I'll feed him again. I want him fat and shiny. Holy Father, (*bows to the baby*) [...] We'll have tea in the palace and I'll learn Italian and the pair of us side by side, launching crusades, banning divorce, denying evolution, destroying the pill, canonizing witches.' (54-5) Carr humorously satirizes the patriarchal exclusivity of Roman Catholic discourse in an absurd comic turn in Curtains' story:

> And they came to a hill where three men were nailing three women
> on three crosses. 'What have we here,' the man said. 'I want
> vinegar,' the one on the middle cross yelled. 'Get me vinegar!'
> 'Would wine do?' the woman asked. 'Has to be vinegar!' the one on
> the cross screamed.

Bender intervenes: 'Oh my God, immaculately receive me', to
which Binder adds, 'Conceive me spectacular'. The segment of
story concludes with all in unison declaring: 'In the name of the
mother, the daughter and the Holy Spirit. *(Pause.)* Ah! *(Pause.)*
MEN!' (50) (The scene at Calvary is one that Carr returns to in *By
the Bog of Cats...* (1998), in which one of the characters, Mrs.
Kilbride, reveals in a surreal twist how her son Carthage built
Calvary for her birthday on the hill behind their house.)

In the play Carr contests the traditional Irish cultural ideology
that 'woman' and 'mother' are innately linked, and powerfully
articulates the increasing void created by the diminished roles of
the traditional hegemonic structures of nationalism, patriarchy and
the church in this country. The playwright's instinctive awareness
of the cultural specificity of gender, sexuality and the body in *Low
in the Dark* can be seen to initiate, as Mary Russo calls it, 'a
dynamic model of a new social subjectivity.'[17] In *The Female
Grotesque: Risk, Excess, Modernity,* Russo writes:

> The re-introduction of the body and categories of the body into the
> realm of what is called the 'political' has been a central concern of
> feminism [...] so that the relation between the symbolic and
> cultural constructs of femininity and woman-ness [...] might be
> brought together towards a dynamic model of a new social
> subjectivity.[18]

Motherhood is a central and ambivalent theme in Carr's plays.
While mother figures are crucial to the dramatic concerns of the
narratives, the naturalized notion of the so-called 'maternal instinct' is repeatedly demythologized. In a distinctly epigrammatical
turn of phrase, Bender says to Binder in Act One, 'I cried. Women

---

[17] Mary Russo, *The Female Grotesque: Risk, Excess, Modernity,* (London & New
York: Routledge, 1994), p.54.
[18] ibid.

always cry when they conceive.' Binder replies, 'No they don't!'
Bender concludes: 'Well they should.' (14) Further on in the
action, Baxter pronounces that pregnancy is 'normal.' The (male)
Bone contemplates this cultural essentialism with a hint of doubt:
'It should be the most natural thing in the world to have a baby.'
(69) When Bone's baby kicks in the womb he asks his partner, 'It's
normal isn't it?', to which Baxter replies, 'Is it not?' The disjointed
quality of Baxter and Bone's discussion denaturalizes or complicates the normative assumptions surrounding pregnancy and
childbirth. Paternity is depicted in a similarly unromantic light in
Low in the Dark. In Act One, when Bender is asked about the
father of her baby, she responds: 'None of your business! Isn't it
enough that he has a father [...] somewhere?' (11) She then writes
a letter to the unknown father: 'My dearest ... My dearest? My
dearest man, I am writing to tell you that you have another son ...'
Binder asks her where she will send the letter: 'Just leave it here.
He'll know it's for him when he comes.' Binder then throws the
letter on the floor: 'He'll never come, they never do.'

Carr's comic and ironic depictions of recognizable character
types, such as 'the nagging wife' and the 'hen-pecked husband',
highlight what John Jervis identifies as:

> the best-known features of othering discourse, namely the
> production of stereotypes [which] simultaneously generalise, exag-
> gerate and fix certain features of particular individual instances to a
> category, thereby rendering them necessary, universal and im-
> mutable features of the category in question.[19]

In Scene Two of Act One, Baxter, who is playing the 'wife' says
to 'husband' Bone (they are both males), '[Y]ou could have buns
every day, and I could knit you a decent scarf'. Bone responds, 'I
hate it when you say things like that! You're only trying to upset
me. (*Points to the wall*) I do everything to please you!'(18)

Everyday activities are made hilariously excessive in *Low in the
Dark* to magnify the preposterous banality of naturalized social
behaviour. In Scene Two of Act One, Baxter, the male who is
playing at being a 'wife', says to 'husband' Bone in a deadpan tone:

---

[19] John Jervis, *Transgressing the Modern*, (Oxford: Blackwell, 1999), pp.8-9.

'I am very happy with you. I cooked you your favourite [...] Two trays! Twenty-four buns all for you.'(18) Baxter then resumes knitting a scarf, which Carr notes to be 'about twenty feet long'. Scaife observes how in performance:

> [t]he knitting of the scarf represented "female action" and it grew longer and longer throughout the play. [...] The lads had a handbag with various items, for when they played the different women in their respective lives, lipstick being of paramount importance to both the men and the women, like war paint in preparation for battle.[20]

Reminiscent in tone of Oscar Wilde's *The Importance of Being Earnest,* itself a carnivalesque parody on the rigidity of Victorian social etiquette and gender divisiveness, a heavily pregnant Bone reminisces on life before children: '(*hand on his stomach*) It was all easier then, I was younger, freer and cheesecake was the thing.'(68) Now married, there is nothing left for Bone to negotiate except one 'bun in the oven' after the next. The whimsical quality of the dialogue echoes Cecily and Gwendolen's excessive deliberations on afternoon tea in Wilde's play. Cecily asks, 'Cake or bread and butter?' Gwendolen replies, 'Bread and butter, please. Cake is rarely seen in the best houses nowadays.'[21] In *Low in the Dark* the newlyweds, Baxter and Bone, have nothing left to negotiate except one 'bun in the oven' after another. In Scene Four of Act One, Carr playfully incorporates the image of the bun as a metaphor for reproduction:

> **Bone:** Darling, you know when you make buns? ...
> **Binder:** 'I'm pregnant,' he says ...
> **Bone:** The temperature has to be just right ...
> **Binder:** 'Are you?' says I, giving him a level look ...
> **Bone:** Has to be 150 degrees ...
> **Binder:** 'Yes,' he whispers, 'must've caught' ...
> **Bone:** And you have to pre-heat the oven ...
> **Binder:** 'And who's the mother,' I'd say, kind of harsh ...
> **Bone:** For fifteen minutes exactly. ...

---

[20] Scaife, p.10.

[21] Oscar Wilde, *The Importance of Being Earnest,* (London: Methuen, 1981), p.49.

Binder: 'Need you ask,' he'd say and the tears would start ...
Bone: Otherwise they don't taste the way they should.
Binder: 'OK! OK,' I'd say, 'I'll stand by you for what it's worth,
but I'm not promising anything, now dry your eyes.' Another bun?
(46-7)

In *The Importance of Being Earnest* Lady Bracknell observes, 'We live,
I regret to say, in an age of surfaces.'[22] Accordingly, Butler asserts
that ' "reality" is not as fixed as we generally assume it to be.'[23] Just
as no-one is who they first seem to be in Wilde's comedy of
manners, identity is continually destabilized through modes of
role-play, inversion and hyperbole in *Low in the Dark.* In Carr's
comedy of bad manners, essentialist socio-cultural myths of gender, sexuality and corporeality are exaggerated and inverted to
'expose the tenuousness of gender "reality" '.[24] With *The Mai* in
1994 comes an end to the conscious experimentation with Absurdist techniques of theatrical form, while distinctive elements of
the surreal and grotesque remain ever present. The Irish landscape of the midlands of Ireland emerges in *The Mai,* where
characters are presented as historically individuated beings rather
than as abstract types, and yet a surreal sensibility is imbued in
figures such as Grandma Fráochlán, and Catwoman and Father
Willow in *By the Bog of Cats....* As Scaife observes:

> The characters [in the later plays] had their beginnings in this
> 'absurd' play and are developed further [...] Marina's sense of fun
> and the ridiculous have been retained despite the seriousness of the
> later subject matter.[25]

While the subversive style and absurdist form of *Low in the Dark*
has been laid aside for now, the subject matter of the later
tragedies displays an organic development from the early works.
As Mac Intyre noted in 1991: '[Marina Carr] has already stated her
theme – love, sex, the erotic. Her attitude seems to be – *What else is
there to write about?*

---

[22] ibid., p.62.
[23] Butler, J, *Gender Trouble*, p.xxiv.
[24] ibid.
[25] Scaife, p.15.

Sources

Bakhtin, Mikhail, *Rabelais and his World,* trans. Helene Iswolsky, (Bloomington: Indiana University Press, 1984).

Barthes, Roland, *The Fashion System,* trans. Matthew Ward and Richard Howard, (New York, 1983).

Butler, Judith, *Gender Trouble: Feminism and the Subversion of Identity*, (New York; Routledge, 1990).

----------- 'Gender Trouble', in *Feminist Theory and the Body: A Reader*, ed. J. Price & M. Shildrick, (Scotland: Edinburgh University Press, 1999).

Carr, Marina, *Marina Carr Plays: One* (London: Faber & Faber, 1999).

----------- Interview with Melissa Sihra (unpublished), Trinity College, Dublin, 25 February 1999.

Esslin, Martin, 'The Theatre of the Absurd', in *The Harcourt Brace Anthology of Drama,* 3rd edition, ed. William B. Worthen (Boston: Thomson and Heimle, 2000).

Garber, Marjorie, 'Cross-Dressing, Gender and Representation', in *The Feminist Reader,* ed. Catherine Belsey and Jane Moore (London: Macmillan Press, 1997).

Jervis, John, *Transgressing the Modern* (Oxford: Blackwell, 1999).

Mac Intyre, Tom, Program Note for *Ullaloo,* Peacock Theatre, March 1991.

Mulvey, Laura, 'Visual Pleasure and Narrative Cinema', in *The Routledge Reader in Gender and Performance,* eds Liz Goodman & Jane de Gay (London & New York: Routledge, 1998).

Russo, Mary, *The Female Grotesque: Risk, Excess, Modernity* (London & New York: Routledge, 1994).

Scaife, Sarahjane, 'Mutual Beginnings: Marina Carr's *Low in the Dark*' in *The Theatre of Marina Carr: before rules was made*, eds Cathy Leeney & Anna McMullan (Dublin: Carysfort Press, 2003).

Wandor, Michelene, 'Cross-dressing, Sexual Representation and the Sexual Division of Labour in the Theatre', in *The Routledge Reader in Gender and Performance*, eds Liz Goodman & Jane de Gay (London & New York: Routledge, 1998).

Wilde, Oscar, *The Importance of Being Earnest* (London: Methuen, 1981).

15 | Notes towards a Foundation for a Theory of Comedy

Alex Johnston

In the autumn of 2000, I began to put together material for a theatre show called *Entertainment*, which took the form of a failed stand-up comedy routine. A short version was performed in the Samuel Beckett Centre for the Pan Pan International Theatre Symposium in January 2001, and a longer version premiered at Dublin's Project Arts Centre in September 2003. These notes come from the process of writing and performing the piece. I'm neither an actor nor a comedian; I'm basically a writer who occasionally performs.

Every discussion of comedy that I've ever read has started with an indulgent little note from the author saying how daft it would be to discuss comedy in a totally serious way, and that therefore he or she hopes the reader finds the following amusing as well as instructive, blah blah blah. Why do they say this? What makes comedy so special? Mightn't it be high time that we started taking comedy seriously? How else are we to work out what it does to us, and how it does it?

My research into the subject has led me to propose two apparently contradictory axioms for further discussion.

Axiom 1: Comedy is a form of verbal and/or conceptual violence. However:

Axiom 2: The basic role of the comedian is to affirm.

What is the point of saying this kind of thing? Let's have a look at the first axiom. Wittgenstein wrote in a notebook:

> Humour is not a mood but a way of looking at the world. So if it is correct to say that humour was stamped out in Nazi Germany, that does not mean that they were not in good spirits, or anything of that sort, but something much deeper and more important ...

> What is it like for people not to have the same sense of humour? They do not react properly to each other. It's as though there were a custom among certain people for one person to throw another a ball which he is supposed to catch and throw back; but some people, instead of throwing it back, put it in their pocket.[1]

If this is right, and to me at any rate this *feels* right, then we can start to picture the sort of thing that goes on when comedy is happening.

The comedian proposes a certain state of affairs, and then almost immediately withdraws the proposal. Result: we laugh. For this to happen, certain conditions must be met:

a) We, the audience, must find the proposed state of affairs not so offensive or unintelligible that we are too shocked or confused by the proposition to consider it for a moment. This is influenced by a combination of factors, which add up to what is sometimes called 'taste', sometimes 'style', and sometimes 'sense of humour'.

b) The comedian must have prepared us in advance to consider the proposal at all. If a stranger walked up to you in the street and started doing a comedy routine at you, you would have reason to feel disturbed, and you could be forgiven for resorting to physical violence. But in the environment of a club or a theatre, it would be okay. This is because of what certain artists began to realize during the latter half of the twentieth century; art is an *expectation* on the part of the viewer/spectator/reader/listener. So what creates the

---

[1] Ludwig Wittgenstein, *Culture and Value*, ed. G.H. von Wright, trans. Peter Winch (Oxford: Blackwell, 1980), pp.78 & 83.

expectation here is the existence of a 'comedy industry', with venues, performers and audiences. The comedian had better withdraw the proposal at the right time or we leave comedy and enter the realm of fiction. This is called 'timing'.

c) It may or may not be true that in dreams begin responsibility, but comedy doesn't give birth to responsibility and insofar as it does, it isn't comedy. Comedy wants to be irresponsible.[2]

In the joke 'Why did the chicken cross the road?', the humour of the punch line ('To get to the other side,' in case you'd forgotten) arises out of the proposition that the chicken might have had some humanly intelligible motive in crossing the road, such as taking its clothes to the launderette or going to a party. We are only encouraged to think in these terms for a second, because this joke is told in a very short time. It's not a very funny joke after the first time you've heard it, but it's a classically simple one, which is maybe why it's become a sort of zero degree of joke, at least for English speakers.

To return to Wittgenstein's example of Nazi Germany, it is well known that the dominant tone of Nazi mass culture and propaganda was one of high, almost tragic seriousness. We can well believe that humour was stamped out, because to joke about the Führer's mission would have been an insult to his dignity. The most striking evidence we have of Nazi humour consists in newsreel footage and photos of SS men forcing Jews to do humiliating menial tasks, while they themselves look on and laugh. This laughter is a perfectly understandable reaction. It is not conventional human behaviour to force old men to clean streets with a toothbrush. Laughter would have eased the tension felt by the SS men and made the whole thing seem normal.[3] But if we had been

---

[2] The reader will notice that I use the word 'comedy' sometimes to mean what stand-up comedians do, and sometimes to refer to a vaguely Northrop Frye-ish notion about a comic as distinct from a tragic mode.

[3] Laughter may also promote health. Clinical studies suggest that production of salivary immunoglobin A (S-IgA), an antibody that fights upper respiratory infections, is boosted by the motor act of laughter. People with a greater capacity to use humour as a way of coping with stress had

watching, we would probably not have found the situation funny at all.

Further evidence that humour accommodates us to the most drastically unrecognizable kinds of behaviour can be found among the Ik people of the Ugandan-Kenyan-Sudanese border.[4] Formerly a tribe of nomads, the Ik were forced by the various governments of the countries between which they travelled to settle permanently in the mountains around the Kidepo valley. They were forbidden to hunt the animals that had always fed them, and forced to become farmers when they knew nothing of farming and had been settled in a dry land with no rain. As a result, the social structure of their tribe completely collapsed. Their entire culture came to revolve around the pursuit and consumption of food by the individual tribesperson. Their word for 'goodness', *marangik*, meant 'the possession of food' and their phrase for a 'good man', *iakw anamarang*, referred to a 'man with a full stomach'. Those who could not feed themselves were despised and rejected. On one occasion, two Ik who had been sent to collect some food aid ate as much as they could of it on the journey home until they actually vomited from overeating, whereupon they ate the rest as well. Nevertheless, the Ik liked a good laugh. One of them, named Giriko, had a son who developed an intestinal blockage. 'At first it amused [Giriko] and he used to call people to look at the boy's distended belly. It was a favourite topic for jokes because finally the boy could neither eat nor drink, since nothing came out that went in.'[5]

The fact that laughter has a function in relieving stress might lead us to speculate whether the point of comedy, of humour, is to create tiny moments of artificial stress that can be instantly relieved. The relief, here, is essential. This is at the root of our second axiom; that the role of the comedian is to affirm.

---

higher levels of S-IgA than more solemn people. See Robert R. Provine, *Laughter: A Scientific Investigation* (Harmondsworth: Penguin, 2001), p.197.

[4] References to the Ik come from Colin Turnbull's *The Mountain People* (London: Picador, 1974).

[5] op.cit., p.180.

I'm suggesting, here, that there has never been a single comedian who did not, on some level, seek the approval of the audience. It could be said that the difference between the comic and the preacher is that the comic needs her audience to identify with her, but the preacher, who seeks to persuade the people that they are unregenerate and must change themselves, starts from the position that the congregation is sufficiently unlike him to need his help. Comedians can preach, but when they do so, they can be striking, insightful, inspiring, boring or irritating but they are not doing the business of comedy. (I use the word 'business' here in the sense of the Business called Show.) Mark Thomas, an apparent exception to this rule in that his entire act consists of political activism but still manages to be funny, in fact fits the model outlined above. He starts from the assumption that his audience thinks the same way that he does, and invites them to laugh at the obstacles placed in the way of political change, and collude in his mischievous attempts to confront authority.

Comedians affirm; affirm what, exactly? The simplest answer would be 'the beliefs and prejudices of the audience', but this appears not to be true in the case of confrontational performers such as Lenny Bruce and Bill Hicks, or out-and-out surrealists like Phil Kay or Jason Byrne. In fact, the two types have more in common than at first appears; they both pay the audience the compliment of assuming that it's sophisticated enough to take whatever the comedian can throw at it. With the surrealist type of comedy, the violence is being done to the audience's accepted notions of comedic grammar, i.e. its acquired expectations about what's funny.[6] Comedy always takes a side, and it has to take the side of the audience, even if the audience hasn't quite realized it yet.[7]

---

[6] Audible proof of this can be found by watching the first few episodes of *Monty Python's Flying Circus* in the order in which they were recorded. The studio audience, like the viewers at home, took several episodes to get used to the Python's disregard for the usual conventions of TV comedy, and the first couple of shows are greeted with only sporadic and slightly embarrassed giggling.

[7] After a performance of *Entertainment* one night a member of the audience came up to me and told me about a comedian he'd seen who punctuated

It could be proposed that the difference between the extent to which the comedian works with the audience's merely superficial beliefs and prejudices, and the extent to which she articulates the audience's inchoate and potentially disturbing (because normally suppressed) inner needs and desires, is the difference between conventional comedy and great comedy. But maybe it's just the difference between light comedy and dark comedy – between Jim Davidson and Lenny Bruce, between a mirror and a CAT scan.

One interesting development in stand-up comedy since the late Seventies is the near-total abandonment by younger comedians of the Joke. Almost Billy Connolly's whole act, in the 1970s, consisted of his telling the kind of jokes he would have heard down the pub when he was a welder. In the 1980s, faced with the challenge of a younger and more adventurous generation, he turned to the more intimate, observational, improvisational comedy that Dave Allen had been doing all along. Jokes have become like standard tunes, staples of popular music until the early Sixties; they're no longer fashionable; but go down your own local or visit certain clubs, and you'll still find them, leading an underground life, battered beyond recognition by drunk amateurs and tired pros. The only other form of circulation left to the joke is as a kind of social interaction, and there are people who actively hate being in joke-telling situations, either because they find listening to jokes boring/pathetic or because they can't tell them properly. This is a

---

his act with a chatty little running commentary based on what he presumed was the audience's reaction: 'Oh dear, that was a little off, dunno about that…oops, bit controversial there…ah well, never mind, you'll like the next bit…' I was intrigued, and I asked the guy, did it work? No, he said, it was horrible; the audience ended up hating the comic, but not for the reasons he seemed to think, and he never seemed to get that he was being booed not because his material was too edgy or uncompromising for the audience, but because he was essentially *apologizing for his own act*, while assuming at the same time a superior position ('This stuff is wasted on you lot but I'm going to do it anyway.') A more disastrous attitude for a performer (any performer) is hard to imagine, and yet it becomes the demeanour of many a comedian who never quite makes it.

pity, since the joke is to urban people something like the folk song is to rural people.[8]

The traditional comedians, the joke-tellers who dominated our TV screens in the 1970s, have been all but frozen out by the younger generation. Some comedians have accepted this with good grace; many have not. The only thing in discussion of comedy that's more boring than joke analysis is the querulous sound of the middle-aged comic bitching about how the younger guys haven't a clue.

They say this because their years of dues-paying have deluded them into believing that they have the secret of comedy – the conviction that they could go into any room and have the audience laughing within minutes. This is the philosopher's stone of comedy, the Universal Laugh, the belief that you can get a laugh out of absolutely anyone. It is possible to demonstrate mathematically that this belief is based more on wishful thinking than on results. Here's how:

> For every ω-consistent recursive class *x* of *formulas* there are recursive *class signs* r such that neither *v* Gen r nor Neg (*v* Gen r) belongs to Flg (*x*) (where *v* is the *free variable* of r).

Maths fans will recognise this as the celebrated Theorem VI of Kurt Gödel's 1931 paper *On Formally Undecidable Propositions of* Principia Mathematica *and Related Systems I*.[9] What Gödel demonstrated in this paper is that formal number systems that aspire to completeness and consistency, such as the kind advanced by Bertrand Russell and A.N. Whitehead in *Principia Mathematica*, will always contain a certain number of statements that are not provable. The wider implication of this is that the more useful a tool (such as a formal number system) is, the more likely it is to be

---

[8] This refers to Ireland, where late-night sessions in the country tend to become occasions for everyone singing a song.

[9] cf. *From Frege to Gödel: A Source Book in Mathematical Logic 1879-1931*, ed. Jean van Heijenoort (Cambridge: Harvard, 1967), p.607. For an extended discussion of Gödel's theorem, see Douglas R. Hofstadter's *Gödel, Escher, Bach: an Eternal Golden Braid*.

incomplete.[10] (A not very strict analogy might be found in mapping. The more detail a map has and the closer it corresponds in scale to the terrain it represents, the less useful it is, because a map that's one-to-one-scale would cover the entire area that it purports to be a guide to.)

Likewise, a comedian who sought to appeal to absolutely every-one would not only have to work very hard indeed, he or she would also be forced to be inconsistent. The same material is not likely to work with a Student Union bar, a Ku Klux Klan meeting and a yurt full of Mongolian tribespeople. From this, we might hypothesize that the effectiveness of comedy depends upon the comedian having some sort of intimacy with the needs and expec-tations of the audience.

Well, duh, says the professional comedian. The winds of change may have blown Bernard Manning off the telly, but his career didn't come to an end, because he knew that there was always an audience for him in his own club, ready to laugh at jokes about women and Pakis. However, to find performers funny, you don't need to share their views. A friend of mine talked of seeing a group of Japanese businessmen on television, laughing their heads off at Manning's act, even when he delivered abusive jokes straight at them; it's entirely possible that they responded more to his amiable smile and the rhythm of his immaculate comic timing than to his material. Oliver Sacks tells a story about two groups of his neurological patients watching a TV broadcast by President Reagan. One group were incapable of understanding body lan-guage but understood the spoken word perfectly well. The other group couldn't comprehend the spoken word but could read the President's body language fine. The former group were totally silent, chilled by Reagan's paranoid fantasies about missile defence, and incapable of being reassured by his folksy manner; the latter group didn't have a clue what he was on about but were laughing their heads off at his carefully judged head-nods and B-movie solemnity.

---

[10] Many philosophers and mathematicians would violently disagree with this interpretation of Gödel's theorem.

Entertainment takes the form of a comedy routine that breaks down early on, and consistently fails the basic rule of comedy – to make the audience laugh. Nevertheless, there were nights during the Dublin run of *Entertainment* when people laughed more or less continuously. These nights were the most satisfying to perform, and I suppose the most conventionally successful performances in that it was nice to feel appreciated, but they were also the least interesting. The most interesting shows were characterized by palpably hostile silence, if not from the entire audience then from one or more members. It was fascinating to see how people reacted when they weren't enjoying the piece on any level; they performed back at me, acting out their own boredom and annoyance with long, loud sighs, over-emphatic fidgeting, tightly folded arms, stony blank faces. Some people fell asleep, or affected to; others leaned back and stared pointedly at the ceiling. (On three consecutive nights, three totally different guys with black ponytails and Lennon glasses sat in the same spot and acted out the same hammy pantomime of umbrage. I started to wonder if they were a *club*.) One night, nobody laughed at all after the first five minutes, and I found that positively exhilarating. It proved, to me at any rate, that while people don't mind being slightly bored as long as a piece exhibits relentless high seriousness (because they think it's probably good for them), they *hate* being bored if they think they're supposed to be laughing. Failed solemnity is indulged; failed comedy is taken personally, and resented.[11]

---

[11] This may only hold true in a society that places a higher value on comedy than on tragedy. I have a theory, anyway, that it's become technically impossible to shock a diehard fringe theatre audience. Effects or actions that would provoke a shock reaction in less self-consciously sophisticated theatregoers are greeted instead by weary disdain and pious head-wagging at what is perceived not as disturbing content but as inept form – a lack of 'ironic distance'. The metropolitan critic can't look like a dork; the clawmarks left on her skin aren't there because the beast was angry, but because the animal tamer wasn't good enough. The hostile criticism of *Entertainment* conformed to this model. Early on, we dropped a heavy hint by dramatising the 'ironic distance' as the tiny gap between two Lego blocks, which I thought would make it unmistakable that ironic distance would be in short supply, but there was still a complaint that

Anyway, comedy came before tragedy,[12] a fact too often forgotten by people who think that seniority confers value.[13] Tragedy arose in Greece out of the conflicts experienced by Athenian democracy. But comedy had long been laughing at the pretensions of those Athenians who wanted to make Athens a more democratic state; its greatest citizen, Pericles, was a frequent target of satire on the stage, as was his intellectual ex-courtesan girlfriend Aspasia. Socrates was a friend of Aristophanes, although at his trial he had the nerve to blame his bad reputation on the influence of the comedians, instead of on his links to the right-wing tyrants who had briefly taken over the city, or his own self-righteous refusal to take part in the most difficult political debates.[14] Socrates was right to feel affronted by the comedians, because in his cranky

---

there wasn't enough of it. Another critic lost the rag entirely and referred to me as 'clever clogs', which I haven't been called since I was eleven. In fact 'spoilsport' would have been more accurate, as well as being something else I haven't been called since I was eleven.

[12] Just to prevent confusion, Eric Weitz has asked me to point out that this refers to comic folk performances; the tragedy competitions in Athens date from the 530s BC, while the comedy competitions came later in the 480s. I would have gone into this more, but I took my *Pelican History of Greece* on holiday to, well, Greece, and I left the damn thing in some taverna.

[13] There was originally a long digression here about the status of comedy in contemporary Irish literature in general, and Martin McDonagh's plays in particular, which I took out because it could be boiled down thus: Martin McDonagh's talent is so impressive that many critics have got a bit carried away, and have tried to make out a case that he is also a serious commentator on the morality of terrorism, writer of moving threnodies about lonely lives, acute observer of Irish life et cetera. This is because critics are embarrassed by comedy and believe that it has a lower status than high seriousness. (Why do you think comic movies almost never win Oscars?) The reasoning goes like this: McDonagh is clearly a brilliant writer – great plays are deep, serious and realistic – McDonagh's plays must be deeper, more serious and more realistic than they appear to be.

[14] cf. *Socrates' Defense (Apology)*, trans. Hugh Tredennick, in *Plato: The Collected Dialogues*, eds Edith Hamilton and Huntingon Cairns (New Jersey: Bollingen/Princeton, 1961), pp.4-5. For a bracing attack on Socrates' hatred of democracy and fondness for right-wing thugs, see I.F. Stone's *The Trial of Socrates* (London: Pimlico, 1997).

and snobbish and self-regarding way he was at least developing and demonstrating a tool – the dialectic – that anyone could use. The earliest comedians whose work survives were conservative and aristocratic, and they were endlessly amused by all those silly clever-clog radicals, with their funny little carry-on about the right of people to vote. Aristophanes' energy and invention have to be considered against his fundamentally conservative outlook.[15] The same volcanic comic creativity can be found in the Tory High Churchman Jonathan Swift. And the tradition of arch-conservative humour goes on; before and during the Second World War, J.B. Morton ('Beachcomber'), a major influence on Dylan Moran, wrote Catholic propaganda and anti-Russian pamphlets, although as George Orwell observed, he stopped producing the latter when the Germans invaded the USSR.[16] Of course, Dylan Moran is neither a Catholic apologist nor a tool of the establishment. But inheritance and influence are things we have little control over.

Radical comedy is much more scarce, because the political or religious radical has better reason to feel more lonely and threaten-

---

[15] It hardly needs to be pointed out that it was only free males who had the vote in Athens, so it wasn't as democratic as all that. Feminist fans of Sparta have pointed out that Spartan women had a lot more political clout than Athenian women; the Spartan code encouraged martial virtue and civic responsibility in men and women alike, even if it was only the men who did the fighting, while Athenian women were expected to stay at home, prepare the dolmades and put up or shut up. This is true, but it needs to be remembered that the Spartans also threw unwanted babies outside the city walls to die. And in one important respect, the Athenian assembly was more democratic than ours; those Athenians who had a vote were able to directly influence the political direction of the polis, instead of being grudgingly allowed to choose which pack of idiots got to run the country. Besides, Aristophanes' wit was not exercised only at the expense of the forces of progress in his own country; he has a dig in *Lysistrata* at the Spartans' reputation for institutionalized sodomy when the Spartan messenger, confronted with the naked female figure of Reconciliation, is only interested in 'ploughing the furrow' between her buttocks.

[16] cf. 'As I Please' 23 June 1944, in George Orwell, *The Collected Essays, Journalism and Letters Volume 3: As I Please 1943-1945* (Harmondsworth: Penguin Books, 1970), p.206.

ed (and therefore, more serious) than the conservative, who after all has the support of the forces of power, capital and reaction. The situation of political humour in the U.S.A. is particularly interesting. There are people in the U.S. media who make a very good living doing humour from a right-wing, pro-imperialist perspective. William F. Buckley blazed the trail back in the Sixties, when on his own chat show he smilingly threatened Noam Chomsky with a punch in the face. When you start from the comforting delusion that there is some sort of Liberal Elite that controls everything, then you can convince yourself that agreeing with whatever the far Right wants is actually pretty damn *fly* and rebellious, even if it entails ridiculing the weak, the defenceless or just anyone who doesn't have a six-figure salary, and even when there are mobile infantry divisions ready to roll over anyone who doesn't laugh. But this peculiarly American type of humour, finding other people's poverty and hardship enormously amusing, has not so far proved exportable.

It could be that tragedy can only occur in a society where power is seriously prepared to consider challenges to its own authority. Somebody, I forget who, once defined tragedy as 'two rights making a wrong', and it's certain that *Antigone* (for example) could only make sense if the audience can accept that Antigone's need to bury her dead has at least equal weight against Creon's insistence on his own interpretation of the law; the two must collide, and it has to end badly for both, or else it's not a tragedy.[17] Comedy will go wherever it can find an audience, but tragedy needs specific circumstances if it's to transcend melodrama or the heritage industry. And this increasing detachment of the comedian from the audience brings us back to the decline of the Joke.

The decline of the Joke in professional stand-up comedy is potentially as significant a cultural phenomenon as the emergence of 'bebop' in the 1940s. Scott DeVeaux has persuasively argued that the early beboppers were driven as much by the desire for

---

[17] Hegel thought that *Antigone* was 'the most excellent and satisfying work of art' of either ancient or modern times. cf. *Hegel on Tragedy* (New York: Anchor Books, 1962), p.74. But then Hegel also thought that Prussia was the perfect state.

professional autonomy, wealth and power – the need to be their own men – as by purely musical considerations.[18] The result was an increased focus on the small group, and on the virtuosity of the individual player, as well as the beginning of the slow decline of the large orchestra. Listeners like Philip Larkin, who had been comfortable with the less harmonically and rhythmically complex jazz of the Twenties, found it difficult to hide their distaste for this development; and as Charlie Parker was followed by Miles Davis and Ornette Coleman and Archie Shepp, the music required increasingly higher levels of knowledge even to understand, let alone play.[19] Something similar has happened with comedy.

Today's received wisdom is that a young comedian must be individual and original, that it's not enough to go up there in a tux and talk about mothers-in-law, but it can be argued that the Joke was able to bring the comic and the audience closer together than the more virtuosic, improvisational comedy required of a young performer today. Of course, the impersonal urbanity of a Jimmy Tarbuck or a Bruce Forsyth at 7pm on a Saturday evening in the 1970s was about as intimate as the transit lounge at Heathrow Terminal 3. But in the telling and reception of the Joke, we are able to contribute to the experience in a way that, sitting in the twentieth row of the Point Depot, we are not.

In a week or so, I'm going to see Eddie Izzard play in Dublin. Besides being a brilliant comedian, Izzard represents the new type of comedy superstar. He is a successful movie actor. He is a celeb-

---

[18] 'The history of jazz can be read, in part, as an attempt by determined musicians to close the gap between artistic ambition and economic reward.' cf. Scott DeVeaux, *The Birth of Bebop – A Social and Musical History* (London: Picador, 1999), p.9 and passim.

[19] This is not a negative criticism of the music; you don't have to understand what Charlie Parker is doing to find him an exhilarating player. But there's no doubt that, as jazz became more codifiable and teachable, it also acquired more and more of the glossy distance of high art, culminating in a player such as Wynton Marsalis, whose technical skill and immaculate sense of what his music needs is, in my opinion, made worthless by the complete absence in his music of the one quality that had fuelled the development of jazz all along: innovation. The equivalent in Irish comedy would be someone like Ed Byrne.

rity, and a photogenic one, thanks to his amiable trans-vestism. He has become internationalized to the point of actually performing his whole routine in a foreign language – his DVD *Circle* features an entire performance *in French*, taped in Paris. For that alone, he should get a subsidy from the EU. I know that the show will be funny, but I also know that it will be effectively unrepeatable to anyone who wasn't there – we will all laugh, and then we will go home. Izzard is a virtuoso comic, but there will be nothing more boring than trying to do his act to other people in the pub after-wards, since his act relies not on sharable experience but on his slightly vague manner, bizarre non-sequiturs, capacity for im-provising in a void, and faultless timing. I realize that what I am really paying for is the ability to *say* that I went to see him, thus enabling me to be one-up on anyone who didn't, but is it really worth it? And if it isn't, what else isn't?

> Yes it is quite funny
> to drink our fill
> so that it burns the throat
>
> the catch is apologetic
> as fun slakes the will
> so far so quite that
>
> and the joke metal turns
> just out of sight
> for ever and ever and ever.
>
> What do you say then
> well yes and no
> about four times a day
>
> sick and nonplussed
> by the thought of less
> you say stuff it.[20]

---

[20] From 'Down Where Changed', in J.H. Prynne, *Poems* (Newcastle: Bloodaxe Books, 1999), p.310.

Contributors

Olabisi Adigun was born in Nigeria and has lived in Ireland for eight years. He is a distinguished workshop facilitator, drummer, storyteller, dramatist and television presenter. He holds a B.A. in Drama (Obafemi Awolowo University), an M.A. in Modern Drama Studies (UCD) and an M.A. in Film/Television (DCU). He is the founder of Arambe Theatre Company in Dublin.

Jim Culleton is the Artistic Director of Fishamble. He has also directed for Pigsback, 7:84 (Scotland), Project Arts Centre, Amharclann de hÍde, Tinderbox, Passion Machine, the Ark, Second Age, the Peacock, Semper Fi, TNL Canada, Scotland's Ensemble @ Dundee Rep, Draíocht, TCD School of Drama and RTE Lyric FM. He has edited and contributed to books for Carysfort Press, Ubu and New Island Books.

Declan Drohan (M.A.. H.Dip.Ad.Ed) lectures in Acting and Performing Arts at Institute of Technology, Sligo. He is a former Course Chair of Drama at the Conservatory of Music and Drama, D.I.T. Rathmines. He is a freelance writer/director/project consultant with a particular interest in the re-imagining of classical texts for contemporary audiences.

David Grant has worked extensively in theatre throughout Ireland as a director, teacher and critic. He has been Managing Editor of Theatre Ireland magazine, Programme Director of the Dublin Theatre Festival and Artistic Director of the Lyric Theatre, Belfast. He has directed more than a hundred theatre productions in contexts ranging from Her Majesty's Prison Maghabery to

London's Royal National Theatre, and is currently Head of Drama at Queen's University, Belfast.

Alex Johnston is a playwright and occasional performer. His writing for theatre includes *Universal Export – Dayshift*, *Entertainment*, which was nominated for Best New Play at the 2004 Irish Times/ESB Theatre Awards; *To Be Confirmed*; *What the Dead Want*; *Royal Supreme*; *Deep Space*; and *Melonfarmer*, which won the 1998 Stewart Parker award. His writing about theatre has appeared in *Performance Research*, *Irish Theatre Magazine* and *The Sunday Times*.

Raymond Keane is a founding member of Barabbas (**www.barabbas.ie**) and is currently Artistic Director. Primarily an actor/theatre-maker/writer/director and clown, his performances have taken him from the back of a truck to the Brooklyn Academy of Music and the big and small screens. He regularly facilitates Barabbas theatre-making workshops both nationally and internationally.

Paul Kennedy has worked as a director, trainer and drama facilitator with Smashing Times Theatre Co Ltd for the past eight years. He has worked with community drama groups in Ringsend, Tallaght, Belfast, Strabane and Derry and has a wide range of professional theatre experience. His play *Desert Places* was produced by the Druid Theatre Co, Galway in August 2000 as part of the Druid Debut Series. He works as a curriculum designer and drama facilitator for Creative Training in Community Drama, a new theatre programmc developed and delivered by Smashing Times and accredited by Queen's University, Belfast. He wrote and directed *Acquainted with the Night* (2002) and *The Tenants* (2003), both presented by Female Parts Theatre Company.

Paul Meade is a writer, director, actor and co-artistic director of Gúna Nua theatre for whom he wrote *Skin Deep* and co-wrote the award-winning *Scenes From a Water Cooler*. From Limerick, Paul trained at the Samuel Beckett Centre, Trinity College, and later received an M.A. in Modern Drama Studies from University College Dublin.

Aoife Monks is a lecturer in theatre in the Department of Film, Theatre and Television at the University of Reading. Aoife's Ph.D. research at Trinity College, Dublin focused on the use of cross-dressing in the work of Deborah Warner and Elizabeth LeCompte, and after completing her doctorate in 2002 she subsequently worked as an intern with the Wooster Group in New York. Aoife is currently working on a monograph on the Wooster Group and an edited book on crossing in contemporary theatre practice.

Mary Moynihan is Assistant Lecturer in Drama at the Dublin Institute of Technology. She is also Artistic director of Smashing Times Theatre Company. She has a B.A. (honours) in Drama and Theatre Studies, from Trinity College, Dublin and an M.A. (honours) in Film Production from the Dublin Institute of Technology. As a professional drama facilitator, Mary has worked with professional and community-based drama groups, women's groups, refugees and asylum seekers and people with disabilities. She is curriculum designer and drama facilitator for Creative Training in Community Drama, a new theatre programme developed and delivered by Smashing Times and accredited by Queen's University Belfast. Mary's plays include *May Our Faces Haunt You, Out of the Outside* and *Silent Screams.*

Anne F. O'Reilly is a lecturer in the Religious Studies Department at St. Patrick's College Drumcondra. She has recently completed her Doctorate at NUI Galway. Her dissertation explored aspects of soul in contemporary Irish drama. She has had a number of articles published in the areas of theology and theatre studies, including articles in *Theatre Stuff* (Carysfort Press, 2000) and *The Theatre of Frank McGuinness: Stages of Mutability* (Carysfort Press, 2003). Her book, *Sacred Play: Soul Journeys in Contemporary Irish Theatre*, is forthcoming from Carysfort Press.

Melissa Sihra is Lecturer in Drama at Queen's University Belfast. She completed her doctoral dissertation on the plays of Marina Carr at the School of Drama, Trinity College in 2002 and has published many articles on Irish theatre. She works as a dramaturg in Ireland and the United States and is currently writing a book on the theatre of Marina Carr.

Bernadette Sweeney is a theatre practitioner and Lecturer in Drama and Theatre Studies at University College Cork.

Jan-Hendrik Wehmeyer lives and works in Dublin. He holds an M.Phil. in Irish Theatre from Trinity College Dublin.

Eric Weitz is a Lecturer in Theatre Studies, Principal Acting Teacher, at the Samuel Beckett Centre, Trinity College Dublin. He holds a Ph.D. in theatre studies from Trinity College Dublin, with research specialities in humour, comedy, and theatre performance. Originally an actor in New York and U.S. regional theatre, he has since taught and directed in the theatre, having founded his own Dublin theatre company, Tricksters.

Rebecca Wilson was a professional actress and dancer in England and founded a small-scale, London Arts Council--funded dance-drama company (Rare Earth). She has taught dance and drama in London under the aegis of ILEA (Inner London Educational Authority). She holds an M.A. (Dist) in Dance Studies from the University of Surrey, an M.A. in Modern Drama Studies from University College Dublin and is currently pursuing a Ph.D. in Melodrama and the Irish Dramatic Tradition at National University of Ireland Galway.

Index

CARYSFORT PRESS

The Press aims to produce high quality publications which, though written and/or edited by academics, will be made accessible to a general readership. The organisation would also like to provide a forum for critical thinking in the Arts in Ireland, again keeping the needs and interests of the general public in view.

Carysfort Press was formed in the summer of 1998. It receives annual funding from the Arts Council.

The directors believe that drama is playing an ever-increasing role in today's society and that enjoyment of the theatre, both professional and amateur, currently plays a central part in Irish culture.

The company publishes contemporary Irish writing for and about the theatre.

Editorial and publishing inquiries to:

CARYSFORT PRESS
58 Woodfield, Scholarstown Road,
Rathfarnham, Dublin 16,
Republic of Ireland
T (353 1) 493 7383 F (353 1) 406 9815
e: info@carysfortpress.com
www.carysfortpress.com

NEW TITLES

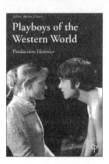

PLAYBOYS OF THE WESTERN WORLD
PRODUCTION HISTORIES
EDITED BY ADRIAN FRAZIER

'Playboys of the Western World is a model of contemporary performance studies.'

'The book is remarkably well-focused: half is a series of production histories of Playboy performances through the twentieth century in the UK, Northern Ireland, the USA, and Ireland. The remainder focuses on one contemporary performance, that of Druid Theatre, as directed by Garry Hynes. The various contemporary social issues that are addressed in relation to Synge's play and this performance of it give the volume an additional interest: it shows how the arts matter.' – Kevin Barry

ISBN 1-904505-06-6
€20

GOETHE AND SCHUBERT
ACROSS THE DIVIDE

Proceedings of the International Conference, 'Goethe and Schubert in Perspective and Performance', Trinity College Dublin, 2003. This volume includes essays by leading scholars – Barkhoff, Boyle, Byrne, Canisius, Dürr, Fischer, Hill, Kramer, Lamport, Lund, Meikle, Newbould, Norman McKay, White, Whitton, Wright, Youens – on Goethe's musicality and his relationship to Schubert; Schubert's contribution to sacred music and the Lied and his setting of Goethe's Singspiel, Claudine. A companion volume of this Singspiel (with piano reduction and English translation) is also available.

ISBN 1-904505-04-X
Goethe and Schubert:
Across the Divide. €25

ISBN 0-9544290-0-1
Goethe and Schubert:
'Claudine von Villa Bella'. €14

CRITICAL MOMENTS

FINTAN O'TOOLE ON MODERN IRISH THEATRE

This new book on the work of Fintan O'Toole, the internationally acclaimed theatre critic and cultural commentator, offers percussive analyses and assessments of the major plays and playwrights in the canon of modern Irish theatre. Fearless and provocative in his judgements, O'Toole is essential reading for anyone interested in criticism or in the current state of Irish theatre.

ISBN 1-904505-03-1
€20

THE THEATRE OF FRANK MCGUINNESS

STAGES OF MUTABILITY
BY HELEN LOJEK

The first edited collection of essays about internationally renowned Irish playwright Frank McGuinness focuses on both performance and text. Interpreters come to diverse conclusions, creating a vigorous dialogue that enriches understanding and reflects a strong consensus about the value of McGuinness's complex work.

ISBN 1-904505-01-5
€15

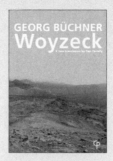

GEORG BÜCHNER: WOYZECK

A NEW TRANSLATION
BY DAN FARRELLY

The most up-to-date German scholarship of Thomas Michael Mayer and Burghard Dedner has finally made it possible to establish an authentic sequence of scenes. The wide-spread view that this play is a prime example of loose, open theatre is no longer sustainable. Directors and teachers are challenged to "read it again".

ISBN 1-904505-02-3
€10

HAMLET

THE SHAKESPEAREAN DIRECTOR
BY MIKE WILCOCK

"This study of the Shakespearean director as viewed through various interpretations of HAMLET is a welcome addition to our understanding of how essential it is for a director to have a clear vision of a great play. It is an important study from which all of us who love Shakespeare and who understand the importance of continuing contemporary exploration may gain new insights."

From the Foreword, by Joe Dowling, Artistic Director, The Guthrie Theater, Minneapolis, MN

ISBN 1-904505-00-7
€18

THEATRE OF SOUND
RADIO AND THE
DRAMATIC IMAGINATION
BY DERMOT RATTIGAN

An innovative study of the challenges that radio drama poses to the creative imagination of the writer, the production team, and the listener.

"A remarkably fine study of radio drama – everywhere informed by the writer's professional experience of such drama in the making…A new theoretical and analytical approach – informative, illuminating and at all times readable."

Richard Allen Cave

ISBN 0-9534-2575-4
€20

THE THEATRE OF MARINA CARR
"BEFORE RULES WAS MADE"
EDITED BY ANNA MCMULLAN
& CATHY LEENEY

As the first published collection of articles on the theatre of Marina Carr, this volume explores the world of Carr's theatrical imagination, the place of her plays in comtemporary theatre in Ireland and abroad and the significance of her highly individual voice.

ISBN 0-9534-2577-0
€20

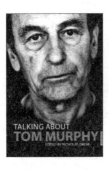

TALKING ABOUT TOM MURPHY
EDITED BY NICHOLAS GRENE

Talking About Tom Murphy is shaped around the six plays in the landmark Abbey Theatre Murphy Season of 2001, assembling some of the best-known commentators on his work: Fintan O'Toole, Chris Morash, Lionel Pilkington, Alexandra Poulain, Shaun Richards, Nicholas Grene and Declan Kiberd.

ISBN 0-9534-2579-7
€10

THEATRE TALK
VOICES OF IRISH THEATRE PRACTITIONERS
EDITED BY LILIAN CHAMBERS, GER FITZGIBBON & EAMONN JORDAN

"This book is the right approach - asking practitioners what they feel."

Sebastian Barry, Playwright.

"... an invaluable and informative collection of interviews with those who make and shape the landscape of Irish Theatre."

Ben Barnes, Artistic Director of the Abbey Theatre

ISBN 0-9534-2576-2
€20

IN SEARCH OF THE SOUTH AFRICAN IPHIGENIE
BY ERIKA VON WIETERSHEIM AND DAN FARRELLY

Discussions of Goethe's "Iphigenie auf Tauris" (Under the Curse) as relevant to women's issues in modern South Africa: women in family and public life; the force of women's spirituality; experience of personal relationships; attitudes to parents and ancestors; involvement with religion.

ISBN 0-9534-2578-9
€10

THE STARVING AND OCTOBER SONG
TWO CONTEMPORARY IRISH PLAYS
BY ANDREW HINDS

The Starving, set during and after the siege of Derry in 1689, is a moving and engrossing drama of the emotional journey of two men.

October Song, a superbly written family drama set in real time in pre-ceasefire Derry.

ISBN 0-9534-2574-6
€10

SEEN AND HEARD (REPRINT)
SIX NEW PLAYS BY IRISH WOMEN
EDITED WITH AN INTRODUCTION BY CATHY LEENEY

A rich and funny, moving and theatrically exciting collection of plays by Mary Elizabeth Burke-Kennedy, Síofra Campbell, Emma Donoghue, Anne Le Marquand Hartigan, Michelle Read and Dolores Walshe.

ISBN 0-9534-2573-8
€20

UNDER THE CURSE

GOETHE'S "IPHIGENIE AUF TAURIS",
IN A NEW VERSION

BY DAN FARRELLY

The Greek myth of Iphigenie grappling
with the curse on the house of Atreus is
brought vividly to life. This version is
currently being used in Johannesburg to
explore problems of ancestry, religion, and
Black African women's spirituality.

ISBN 0-9534-2572-X
€8.25

URFAUST

A NEW VERSION OF GOETHE'S EARLY
"FAUST" IN BRECHTIAN MODE

BY DAN FARRELLY

This version is based on Brecht's irreverent
and daring re-interpretation of the German
classic.

"Urfaust is a kind of well-spring for German
theatre... The love-story is the most daring
and the most profound in German
dramatic literature." *Brecht*

ISBN 0-9534257-0-3
€7.60

THEATRE STUFF (REPRINT)

CRITICAL ESSAYS ON CONTEMPORARY
IRISH THEATRE

EDITED BY EAMONN JORDAN

Best selling essays on the successes and
debates of contemporary Irish theatre at
home and abroad.

Contributors include: Thomas Kilroy, Declan
Hughes, Anna McMullan, Declan Kiberd,
Deirdre Mulrooney, Fintan O'Toole,
Christopher Murray, Caoimhe McAvinchey
and Terry Eagleton.

ISBN 0-9534-2571-1
€19

HOW TO ORDER

TRADE ORDERS DIRECTLY TO

CMD
Columba Mercier Distribution
55A Spruce Avenue
Stillorgan Industrial Park
Blackrock
Co. Dublin

T (353 1) 294 2560
F (353 1) 294 2564
E cmd@columba.ie

or contact
SALES@BROOKSIDE.IE